AMERICANA

Dic Edwards

AMERICANA
UTAH BLUE
OVER MILK WOOD
Poems

OBERON BOOKS
LONDON

Utah Blue first published in 1995 by Made In Wales Stage Company.

This anthology first published in 2000 by Oberon Books Ltd. (incorporating Absolute Classics)
521 Caledonian Road, London N7 9RH
Tel: 020 7607 3637 / Fax: 020 7607 3629

e-mail: oberon.books@btinternet.com

ISBN: 1 84002 159 4

Cover design: Andrzej Klimowski

Typography: Richard Doust

Back cover photograph: Tony Unsworth

Printed in Great Britain by Antony Rowe Ltd, Reading.

Contents

Acknowledgements

Thanks to Amanda for the typing

Thanks to Steve and Spectacle for their support

Thank you to the Department of Theatre, Film and
Television Studies, Aberystwyth University

Thanks to Gilly Adams for commissioning *Utah Blue*

Utah Blue was supported by the Welsh Arts Council

Introduction

Dic Edwards

My plays are often about what I call *the evicted* – the outsider, yes, and perhaps something more poignant and even pathetic: like someone waiting in the street outside their home, waiting to be called back in. I don't offer solutions to their problems: I don't get them back in. My anger with their condition is, hopefully, what drives my dramatic purpose.

Both these plays are about eviction. Geniuses, perhaps, if genius lives outside The Law. The one, Gary Gilmore was real, the other, Mr. Pugh fictional in the immediate sense though clearly an evocation of his own first originator, Dylan Thomas.

Gary Gilmore killed two men – Mormon boys – for even less reason than a bad one and went on to insist the State carry out the death penalty it had imposed on him. Gary Gilmore wants to die for America. Pugh, like Dylan, has come to America to die.

Dylan was a great poet – one of the century's finest – yet he is best remembered for a radio play about which the Thomas authority Walford Davies has said: 'its quality is best appreciated when we concede its essentially low-key ambitions.'[1] It's the impossibility of Welshness for Dylan that, paradoxically, gives *Under Milk Wood* its reputation. And this misleadingly high status has been responsible for evicting Thomas from his own canon: an anomaly encouraged by Wales itself. It's not possible for the master to belong to a culture which so blatantly exploits itself. Just as it's not possible for Pugh to belong to Thomas's play in my own. So he flees not only the curse put on him by Thomas's play but the culture which ultimately evicted Dylan by so eulogising his less than best effort.

Gary Gilmore could have been an artist. A painter. It's said he was good. But his culture, Mormonism, which helped destroy the art in him and make the monster is a powerful evicting force as is that distant cousin of Mormonism, Welsh non-conformism, a notion which, as Walford Davies points out, Dylan draws our attention to in the Reverend Eli Jenkins' ironic and satirical 'Llareggub Hill, that mystic tumulus…'[2] speech, and which is implicit in Pugh's inordinate reaction to a mooted, murderous thought posited in a fictional text. In the end, both these religions closeted within their respective cultures, kill art. Utah is Wales displaced.

If genius is the arriving at the right place at the right time in a way that radically challenges our perception of things then Gary Gilmore was *the* perverse genius (his campaign to get the authorities to kill him and the consequent proliferation of execution, has allowed the world to see the true murderous nature of America's death laws: these days they execute children – mostly black – which Gary anticipates in his 'coming up towards Atlanta with Lee's boys…' speech). Gary's genius was to damn himself; Pugh is damned by the fictional echoes of Dylan's own real genius which damned Dylan himself and which ironically and, perhaps, perversely, has shown the universe the true nature of Welsh culture which Dylan in his own lifetime, like Pugh, was cast out from.

If you want to write *out* of Wales (as *Mrs* Walford Davies puts it), just as if you want to paint out of Utah – you experience the intolerable pressure of apparently owed acknowledgments demanded by those who impose duties on expression. Gary's mother calls them the Dead Makers. Here we might call them The Preachers – those who would give voice to Pugh's demons.

America is a stopping off point for my drama: it's where the evicted go – somewhere out there in Willy Loman's 'blue' – to sort things out before (unless they stay) returning for the reckoning.

Dic Edwards
London 2000

[1] Walford Davies – *Dylan Thomas*, University of Wales Press, 1990, P.52

[2] Ibid, P.54

UTAH BLUE

scenes in a culture of murder

for Steve Davis

Characters

GARY
MIKAL
NICOLE
BESSIE

The world premiere of *Utah Blue* was presented by Made In Wales Stage Company at The Point, Cardiff on 22 February 1995, with the following cast:

GARY, Dorian Lough

MIKAL, Andrew Howard

NICOLE, Linda Quinn

BESSIE, Hilary Beckett

Director, Michael McCarthy

Designer, Sue Pearce

Lighting Designer, Nick Macliammoir

Production Manager, Tim Rich

Deputy Stage Manager, Leanne Marlborough Rochefort

Assistant Stage Manager, Frances Allsworth

For Made In Wales

Artistic Director, Gilly Adams

Administrator, Donna Gower

Press/Publicity, Nicola Russell/Penny Simpson

Gary's speech to judge at 1974 trial

"I would like to make a special appeal for leniency. I've been locked up the last 9½ calendar years and I have had about 2½ years of freedom since I was 14 years old. I have always gotten time and always done it, never been paroled. I've never had a break from the law, and I have never asked for a break until now. Your honour, you can keep a person locked up too long just as you can keep them long enough. What I am saying is there is an appropriate time to release somebody or give them a break...if you were to grant me probation on this sentence, you wouldn't be turning me loose right now. I still have additional time, but like I said, I have got problems, and if you give me more time, I'm going to compound them."

The judge sentenced him to nine additional years.

Taken from *The Executioner's Song* by Norman Mailer.

Set Notes

The main feature of the set is two beds. These are used variously to describe different locations: Gary and Mikal's family home, Bessie's trailer; Mikal's flat; Gary's prison cell etc.

Note about Gary and Gary's body

Gary should wear the executioner's 'mark' on his chest throughout this part in the play.

Gary's Body should be dressed in a white body stocking. There are holes in the stocking with stains where the blood has run down from the holes. There is a small cluster of holes above the heart [maybe 3] and one or two others.

PART ONE

Scene 1

Nicole bringing it all back home

NICOLE comes on in work clothes. She flops onto one of the beds.

NICOLE: (*To the audience.*) I'm just so fucked with that job!
I have to use a power sewing machine. They sent me to
school for a week to learn how to use it. But you need
co-ordination and my head! I'm always so bombed out!
They put me on this one machine and just when I'm
getting the hang of it they put me on another! And then
that one fucks up just when I'm least expecting it.
So, this is the condition I'm in the night I meet Gary.
Been married three times, two kids; have not slept with
anyone for weeks but don't care because I have a house
which is better than a man! And I'm not even twenty!
I'm with my sister-in-law cruising in my mustang trying
to wind down and we call in on my cousin, and there's
this strange-looking guy sitting on the couch.
(*GARY comes on and sits on the bed.*)
(*To the audience.*) No one bothers to introduce us so I
ignore him, but then our eyes meet and he says:

GARY: I know you.

NICOLE: (*To the audience.*) Something flashed through my
mind but then I thought: no, I never met this guy before,
then, after a few minutes he looks at me again and says:

GARY: Hey, I know you!

NICOLE: (*To the audience.*) I said; 'Yeah, maybe.' I thought
about it a moment then said again: 'maybe'. I thought:
'Maybe I know him from another time'. I was scared of
what I was getting myself into. I wasn't afraid of him,
I was scared. I was afraid of getting caught up with
another loser. Just as I was getting ready to go he says:

GARY: Give me your phone number.

NICOLE: (*To the audience.*) I didn't want to give the impression I was easy...

GARY: (*To the audience.*) So she says:

NICOLE: No!

(*GARY sits next to NICOLE.*)

GARY: (*To the audience.*) I was fucking amazed, man! 'No'!

NICOLE: (*To the audience.*) He said:

GARY: It don't make sense. You walk outta here and I'm never going to see you again! (*To the audience.*) Then she said:

NICOLE: I won't give it to you, I went and – shit! By the time I was outta the door I was screaming 'cos I wanted him to have that number so bad! I didn't even have a phone! I'd have to give my next-door neighbour's. So I drove home and drove back again.

GARY: (*To the audience.*) And it wasn't long before you got to saying:

NICOLE: Ever since I was a kid I've believed in reincarnation. It's the only thing that makes sense. You have a soul and after you die your soul comes back to life as a new baby. You got a new life where you suffer for what you done wrong in your past life. (*To the audience.*) And I was amazed when he said:

GARY: Karma, I've believed in it for a long time. Punishment is having to face something you haven't been able to face in this life.

NICOLE: (*To the audience.*) Then he said – which really scared me:

GARY: If you murdered somebody you might have to come back and be the parents of that person in a future century. That's the whole point of living. Facing yourself, if you don't, the weight gets bigger.

NICOLE: (*To the audience.*) I thought: shit! This is the best conversation I've ever had! Then he sat right next to me...

GARY: (*To the audience.*) And I held her face in my hands. (*He does this.*)

NICOLE: (*To the audience.*) And he said:

GARY: Hey, I love you!

NICOLE: (*To the audience.*) And I thought: 'O, Jesus! I hate "I love you". I've said it so many times when I didn't mean it! Still, I suppose now I have to say it...'

GARY: (*To the audience.*) So she says:

NICOLE: I love you. (*To the audience.*) But it sounded shit. Wrong echo. Then he says:

GARY: Hey, there's a place in the darkness. You know what I mean?

NICOLE: (*To the audience.*) Then it wasn't long before he said:

GARY: I don't want just to fuck you, I want to make love to you.

NICOLE: (*To the audience.*) And it wasn't long before...
(*NICOLE lays on the bed. GARY gets on top of her. He pumps away at her.*)
(*To the audience.*) There he was, pumping away but he'd drunk too much and couldn't get a hard-on. He wouldn't stop and rest. He just kept going. He looked like he'd been hit with a tyre lever. After a while he said...

GARY: (*To the audience.*) You got to help me baby.

NICOLE: (*To the audience.*) So I did what I could.
(*They turn over and NICOLE puts her head between GARY's legs and moves it back and forth.*)
(*To the audience.*) But my neck just got tired...

GARY: (*To the audience.*) She said:

NICOLE: Let's just cool it for a while. (*To the audience.*) Then he said:

GARY: Get on top of me. (*Pause.*) I asked you gently.

NICOLE: Yeah, you did, I know.
(*She gets on top of him and moves.*)
(*To the audience.*) I tried but it was no good. (*To GARY.*) You just kept saying:

GARY: It's the beer, baby. The beer and the Fiorinal, which I gotta take every day for my headache.
(*She stops.*)

NICOLE: (*To the audience.*) And it got so that when things weren't good they were always like this.
(*She gets off him.*)

(*To the audience.*) In the end it got to be mostly like this. In the end it just made him so mad!

(*They sit in silence. They begin to speak together.*)

GARY: It was the…

NICOLE: (*To the audience.*) Everything happened so quick! He shoots those two guys, then he says they gotta shoot him, then they shoot him.

(*GARY is rubbing his hands together with his head hanging as if remorseful.*)

GARY: I fucked up baby.

NICOLE: Yeah, you did! What was all that karma shit? It doesn't make sense!

(*To the audience.*) And he keeps saying:

GARY: It was the Fiorinal!

NICOLE: (*To the audience.*) And I say: (*To GARY.*) 'Fuck that Gary! Blaming a dumb fucking drug!'

GARY: Hey! But who am I? I didn't make myself! I came outta my mother's womb! I came outta Utah!

(*Lights down.*

NICOLE goes, GARY gets onto bed. BESSIE comes on.)

Scene 2

Bessie Gilmore is subject to her history

BESSIE is standing over the body of GARY. On his chest, over his heart, there is a marker which has been shot through by bullets.

BESSIE: (*Tearfully.*) This is how it is. This is what it is. There is no other way that it is. This is what is. This is the way. This is the way it is with Gilmores. Gary dead is the way it is. Gary not dead is not the way it is. This is the only way it is. God is. The Mormon Church is, Gary is. Dead. The world is. Utah is. The United States of America is. The bullet is. And the other bullet is. The hole is. In Gary. Gary's life is. Not. Gary is. Dead. This is how it is.

(*Silence.*

GARY'S BODY begins to speak gently. Child-like.)

GARY'S BODY: (*Troubled.*) Ma?

(*Pause.*

GARY'S BODY suddenly sits upright in bed as though he'd just woken from a bad dream. He looks like a dead man. He speaks with his eyes closed.)

I had a nightmare. About being beheaded! Ma! Ma!

(*GARY'S BODY lays back down.*

Silence.)

I was with my brigade. We was coming up towards Atlanta with Lee's boys. There was this small shack. Hut. In it was a black family. Just a woman, old guy and little kids. I fired it Ma! Just burnt it the hell down. Killed all them little black kiddies! I told Nicole I did something bad! Just knew it! Christ Ma! Should execute every white bastard that could kill them little black kiddies! I told Nicole!

(*Silence.*)

BESSIE: I couldn't have done nothing. I said I could. I said if I could've got to Provo, Gary wouldn't've killed those boys. Those Brigham Young boys. It wasn't the other end of the earth! I could've gone! But I couldn't've done nothing. I couldn't've done nothing because it's not up to me to do it. This boy wanted to be a priest when he was nine and this happens! So how could I do anything! Locked up all his life, instead of learning, he was locked up! Couldn't work for a living nor pay a bill. So how could I have done something? Anything?

(*GARY'S BODY suddenly starts laughing outrageously.*)

GARY'S BODY: There was this guy in the pen! Fungoo. He loved me. Strong and dumb. He asked me to make a rosebud on the back of his neck. I took out my needle and my India ink and instead of a rosebud, I tattooed a real skinny little dick on him with peanut-sized balls. (*Laughing outrageously.*) His ma and dad were coming next day. When he found out what I'd done he had to see his folks with a towel wrapped around his neck even though it was over a hundred! Said he liked to wear a towel in the heat!

(*GARY'S BODY laughs so much it sits up – but still with eyes closed.*)

19

Fungoo was so dumb he wouldn't get mad at me! Just said: Gary, I can't go round with a pecker on my neck! (*Laughing.*) Okay, I said: I'll make it into a snake. Instead, I made it into a big, three-headed cock that had the ugliest warts you ever laid your eyes on! I couldn't hardly stop laughing all the while I was doing it! Fungoo was saying: make sure it's a nice snake! I said to him: O, I believe this is the most beautiful thing I ever seen! I guess I must have racked up some real bad karma on that one but I just couldn't resist it! Always been like that. I gotta be a hero! Just like a kid. Like I never growed up. Like I had to be a hero for Nicole!

(*Silence.*

GARY'S BODY lays back down.)

BESSIE: (*Suddenly wailing loudly.*) How do I save Mikal from all this?

GARY'S BODY: (*Suddenly crying out.*) Ma! Mummy! I couldn't find Nicole! I looked all over Ma!

BESSIE: I can't do nothing!

GARY'S BODY: Hey Ma! Remember my paintings? I am an artist!

BESSIE: Nothing! Now I'm so old, so decrepit they play the band when I get out into the street! Mikal! You gotta break out yourself son!

GARY'S BODY: Ma! One of those guys shot me in the mouth! As if to say: 'that Gary Gilmore always had too much to say. He had a big mouth and I'm gonna shut it!' So he didn't shoot me in the heart where he's s'posed to...he shot me in the mouth! (*Tearfully.*) Right through my whole brain! D'you think it'll affect me for when I come back Ma? Why'd that guy have to do that? He was just a nobody! A nobody I done nothing to!

(*Silence.*

Lights down.)

Scene 3

We live in a culture of murder

GARY and MIKAL's bedroom. 1960s.

BESSIE gets into her bed. GARY and MIKAL are lying either end of the bed. They are both looking to the ceiling.

GARY: You asleep Mikey?

MIKAL: No.

GARY: Okay. Here's something: You ever heard of a guy called Spinoza?

MIKAL: What is he a con?

GARY: No, Christ! A philosopher! Jesus! Anyway, he reckoned everything was one thing.

MIKAL: I don't get it Gary.

GARY: One thing! Like...like a woman. A woman is one thing. You can love her, hate her, screw her, dump her, pick her up again, get her to wash your socks or suck your cock! Ha, ha!

MIKAL: Shurrup Gary! Ma'll hear you.

GARY: You can pray for her or pray to her. On your knees man! You can live for her or die for her. It's all there in one thing.

MIKAL: I still don't get it.

GARY: The universe! Everything is in one thing. That's what he said. It's all one substance and we're all just different bits of the one substance.

MIKAL: Yeah?

GARY: So if I die I'm not dead. I could only be dead if the whole substance died.

MIKAL: This substance sounds like a truckload of horseshit!

(*GARY kicks MIKAL under the bedclothes.*)

GARY: Hey! Don't take the Micky, Mikey!

MIKAL: Ha, ha. You're crazy Gary! I love you! Stop kicking me!

GARY: You're lucky I don't stick my toe up your butt even though you are my kid brother.

MIKAL: I think that would be illegal!

GARY: Yeah! And I'm law-abiding. So pay attention because I don't want to become a social misfit!

MIKAL: Okay.

GARY: Spinoza?

MIKAL: Yeah, okay.

GARY: Where was I?

MIKAL: The substance.

GARY: O, yeah, I could only be dead if the whole substance died. Which would mean that you and everything else would be dead. Think that's neat?

MIKAL: I think it's depressing Gary! Last thing at night.

GARY: Don't be crazy Mikey! I'm describing salvation! I'm describing heaven. I'm describing the government and the state rules. This way shows why wars are okay. Because you're not killing fifty million people you're just changing a feature of the substance.

MIKAL: But that's like saying it's not possible to murder anyone! That people who're murdered may die in a way but then they just get soaked up in the substance.

GARY: Well how d'you think they figure out execution? Eh? It's because when they execute somebody it's as a result of him going out and fiddling with the substance; rearranging it to satisfy his own personal habits say…

MIKAL: You mean topping someone.

GARY: You see? You use gruntly words but it's not like that! It's like…it's like water, Hey Mikey, you want a piss?

MIKAL: Na.

GARY: Good.

(*GARY picks up a mirror.*)

Squeeze out a couple of drops onto that.

MIKAL: What?

GARY: Onto the mirror! Squeeze out a couple of dropsa piss.

MIKAL: What for?

GARY: I want to show you an experiment.

MIKAL: Wouldn't water do?

GARY: Yea, but we haven't got any water!

MIKAL: Christ, Gary! Go to the bathroom!

GARY: Jesus kid! I'm not going all the way down there.
Do it, will you?

MIKAL: (*Reluctantly.*) Okay.
(*MIKAL prepares to do it.*)
And what if I suddenly can't stop? What if I open up the
floodgates?

GARY: Then you're going to get one strangled pecker boy!
(*They laugh.*)
Hey, mind you don't piss yerself!
(*They laugh more.*)

MIKAL: Gary, I can't do this! I'm cracking up! I'm going
to piss all over the bed!

GARY: You sound like a fuckin' recidivist, man! Just think
of something real mean.

MIKAL: Like what?

GARY: Like...your mother's pussy.

MIKAL: (*Suddenly angry.*) Hey, I hate that! There's no need
for it.

GARY: You done it?
(*Pause.*)

MIKAL: Yeah.

GARY: So it worked!
(*GARY takes the mirror.*
MIKAL gets back into bed.)
Look at this.
(*They look over the mirror in the middle of the bed.*)
Two pieces of piss. One big, one small. Tip the mirror a
bit and...see? The little bit joins with the big bit!
The big bit takes it in. It's nature. That little bita piss
was the equivalent of a murderer. What happened to the
little bit of piss? It got made part of the substance again.
And that's just what happens with the murderer.

MIKAL: You mean when they execute him?

GARY: Yeah. He ain't going to come back in no other way.
(*Pause.*) You know what the substance is?

MIKAL: What? Jees Gary I'm getting tired now!

GARY: God.

MIKAL: God.

GARY: Yeah. The substance is God. And we're all part of it so we're all part of him. Which means if we're all part of God we must be partly gods ourselves. Take a look under the bedclothes.

(*MIKAL does.*)

MIKAL: Ha, ha, Gary! You're sick!

GARY: Wouldn't you say that was a God-like stalk?

MIKAL: Anyway, what's the point in God if we're all gods? Especially if you're one?!

GARY: O, I forgot. The gods are the people who can change the nature of the substance.

MIKAL: How?

GARY: By a deliberate, singular, highly original action. Something without a motive. Without a mundane motive that is. The action is carried out only because the person carrying it out wants it carried out. No other reason.

(*Pause.*)

MIKAL: Sounds like you're talking about murder again.

GARY: Well, maybe. Only not any ordinary murder. Something like Charley Manson did when they cut up Sharon Tate. Or the way he made that chick Squeaky Fromme take a pot-shot at President Ford even though he was nowhere near her. Anything big and original.

MIKAL: So these people, murderers and the rest, are like little gods who have to be brought back to the big God?

GARY: Yeah! You learn quick! I couldn't've put it better.

(*Pause.*)

MIKAL: I think it's scary.

(*Pause.*)

GARY: Here's another thing: this guy Spinoza, all he did all his life was he made glasses. Just sat in his little room all day and night and just went right on making those glasses.

MIKAL: How?

GARY: He'd grind the glass. That's how you do it. Only here's something: it almost made him blind. Grinding glass so that others can see who probably only want to spend their days looking at shit. Life in the substance, man. This guy looking out on infinity grinding glass into infinitesimal curves which will blind him.

MIKAL: You know, that's almost like a poem Gary. How do you know so much?

GARY: From endless nights in the pen when I can't go to sleep…

MIKAL: (*With a sigh.*) Like now?

GARY: Yeah. But also…also because, kid, I walk with death. I walk with death.

MIKAL: Jesus! Why'd you say such miserable things!

GARY: No, listen! When I was a kid, death would whisper into my ear at night. That's how I got to sleep. And as I grew up, death would walk with me to school. Yeah! In school I learned with death; in the playground I played with death; when I played hookey, I played hookey with death. Death was in my school-bag; in my lunchbox; in my pencil case; with my paint brushes. Death came down the chimney at Christmas and death lit up the Christmas tree. I ate at the table with death and left the table with death. When I was a baby I cuddled death. I sucked on death's teat. (*Pause.*) I saw death in my judges and death in my juries and death in my screws. When I went to the gas station I was with death; when I went to a motel I was with death. When I humped a chick I was with death and when I kissed I was with death. Death taught me love. Death taught me life. Death taught me to see just as death taught me to paint. I was death's artist.

(*Silence.*)

You don't believe me? Hey? Get Ma to tell you a bedtime story. Yeah?

MIKAL: Shurrup Gar. I got to get to sleep.

GARY: You don't want to call her? Okay. I'll call her. Ma! Ma!

(*BESSIE gets out of her bed. She is now much younger.*)

BESSIE: Gary?

GARY: Ma, tell us the story about when you were a kid. About the Dead Makers.

BESSIE: This time of night?

GARY: I can't sleep!

MIKAL: That's 'cos he keeps talking Ma!
 (*GARY kicks MIKAL playfully.*)
GARY: Yeah. Well I won't talk if I gets a bedtime story.
 Will I, you jerk-off!
MIKAL: Hey Ma! Tell him!
BESSIE: Okay, settle down boys.
 (*Pause while GARY and MIKAL settle down.*
 As BESSIE speaks the lights go down.)
 One morning, about fifty years ago, at winter time, my
 Pa loaded us all, me and my brothers and sisters into the
 family wagon and drove us in darkness. To a hanging.
GARY: I like the way ya stopped there Ma, between 'drove
 us in darkness' and 'to a hanging'.
MIKAL: Ma!
BESSIE: Gary!
GARY: Okay, okay! I won't say another word!
BESSIE: I watched the man being led up the stairs to the
 noose and the executioner. But I would not watch the
 hanging! I just shut my eyes tight and buried my face
 in my Pa's side. Then I heard the trap-door crack open
 and the horrible snapping sound as the man went down
 and his head broke off at the neck. There was cheers
 and applause. As I moved away from the site I turned
 back and saw the man's body dangling and swaying.
 Men were holding the hands of their children, pointing
 at the corpse. 'Remember this moment' they were
 saying. Happily. I hate those men. I call them the
 Dead Makers. Mormons believed that the bloodier
 executions were, the better. Death by firing squad or
 death by hanging. No other death was allowed. For the
 hangings they'd put the gallows in meadows in valleys
 and the Mormons would bring their families to watch.
 Mormons had been so persecuted that they came to
 BELIEVE in violence. They used violence for protection
 but it got that they also used violence for vengeance and
 punishment.
 (*Pause.*)
GARY: And just used violence, full stop! Look at all the
 guys who've kicked the shit out of you Ma!

BESSIE: Gary!

GARY: It's true! Your Pa, your husband!...

MIKAL: Gary, shut up!

(*Silence.*)

BESSIE: Before you were born, Mikal, when the other boys were growing up, we would sit around the table and write letters to any governors of states where there were boys to be hanged begging for mercy. Frank, Junior, Gaylen and Gary all wrote those letters.

GARY: I never begged for mercy! Why'd you say that? Now you spoilt the story! I'm going to sleep!

(*Pause.*)

BESSIE: Mikal? You alright?

(*Silence.*

Lights are down.

GARY suddenly sits bolt upright in bed yelling and screaming. He is holding his neck.

MIKAL wakes confused.)

MIKAL: Gary! What is it?

BESSIE: (*In the dark.*) What is it son?

GARY: (*Calmly.*) Nothing. (*Pause.*) Nothing. I dreamed. I dreamed I had my head cut off. That's all.

(*Silence.*

Lights down.)

Scene 4

Each of Bessie's children was her last chance

Light on BESSIE. Some years later.

BESSIE: I think in life there are just days. The day I got taken to the hanging was a big day. Another big day was when Frank, my husband, hit me. And when Gary was born. I remember seeing him reach out to touch that child but almost he couldn't do it. I saw how the bloom on my boys went. I think about my father and my mother. She was paled by him. I was never going to be like that. No one was going to pale my life like that.

I fought it. I always fought it. He was colourful, my husband, funny, he was warm. He was beautiful. And the boys were beautiful boys, Gary was a beautiful boy. Frank Jnr., he wasn't such a beautiful boy, but Mikal, he was a beautiful boy. I grieve for Gary being like he is.
(*GARY gets up out of darkness.*)

GARY: What do you mean you grieve for me?

BESSIE: So many times in jail? You spent most of your life in jail, son!

GARY: Well why you blamin' me for Chrissakes? I didn't get me born! I didn't get me brung up! I didn't put the rat in my brain! I didn't make it rain on days it was supposed to be sunny! I didn't tell myself there was nothin' I could do about nothin'! I didn't make society! I didn't make the streets so as you had to have cops on them!

BESSIE: But you're a painter! I've seen the pictures!
(*MIKAL gets up.*)

MIKAL: What's all the hollering?

BESSIE: He paints children!

MIKAL: Yeah, I know I seen them. So what's all the hollerin'?

GARY: You know what Mikal, you fart in your sleep! You must be the fartiest bastard I ever knew!
(*MIKAL looks bemused.*)

MIKAL: What?

GARY: Farting! You get it in the can. All the time. There's guys in there can out-fart *Le Petomain* but I don't expect it at home.

MIKAL: What is this?

GARY: You! It's like you been singing songs all night with your arse! Why don't you save it up for a week and make an album! Become a fart artist!

MIKAL: Jesus, Gary, why can't you ever take anything serious? Why don't you ever grow up before you get too old?

GARY: Grow up? I don't want to grow up. That way I can remain innocent. See?

BESSIE: He paints children with big eyes! So beautiful.

GARY: Yeah, and I paint pictures of the dead. So what's the big deal? Maybe I should paint the biggest painting ever. Only not with a brush…

(*GARY aims his hand in a gesture of a gun.*)

MIKAL: You're crazy Gary! Why'd you want to give us that shit?

GARY: She started it!

MIKAL: She's your mother, man!

BESSIE: (*Tearfully.*) Gary, you scare me to death! I never been able to keep the night from my life, and maybe not yours. I want only one thing now; that for Mikal it's different.

(*BESSIE gets into her bed.*)

GARY: (*To MIKAL.*) Why? D'you want to be an artist?

MIKAL: Yeah.

GARY: Forget it.

MIKAL: What?

GARY: There's no such thing.

MIKAL: It's what you do! Your paintings are too much! Everybody says it!

GARY: (*Angry.*) Hey get this! You want to learn how to be an artist? Learn to eat pussy! That's the only art that matters. You think that this world we live in gives a shit about art? When I was in the slammer man, there was a cat in there who was an artist. You know what he could do? He could suck his own dick! He was the ultimate performance artist. And also: he murdered with precision. With delicacy. And with the detail of Van Eyck. He is revered by society for his dexterity in the latter department because baby you are living in a culture of murder. One day I'll show you. I will commit the ultimate work of art and you'll see. That guy, the dick-sucker was a most successful member of society. He conformed to all that society expected of him. You want to be an artist? Learn to eat pussy. Keep your head down.

(*He takes hold of his own crotch with violence.*)

Get me? You don't want it blown off. That's the real art.
Save getting your head blown off. Unless… (*Pause.*) Shit!
(*MIKAL takes some paintings from under the bed.*)

MIKAL: I don't believe you Gary. That's all bullshit.
What about these?
(*MIKAL puts the paintings and drawings carefully
before him.*
GARY pauses.
MIKAL is looking through the paintings with reverence.)
They're beautiful Gary. You're a real artist.
(*GARY snatches the paintings.*
He is in a sudden uncontrollable rage.
He rips up the paintings and throws them around.
MIKAL cries.)
Gary!

GARY: I said they're nothing!
(*GARY kneels astride MIKAL.*
He raises a fist above him.)
You're not learning kid!
(*GARY struggles with himself beating his chest and yelling out.*
MIKAL cries.)

MIKAL: No Gary! Stop it! Stop it!

GARY: I said eat pussy! Eat pussy! Just eat! Eat!
(*GARY gets up.*)
I'll give you a work of art!
(*GARY goes off.*
Lights down.)
(*Off.*) This one's for Nicole.

MIKAL: Who's Nicole?!
(*Sound of gunshot.*)
Gary!

GARY: (*Off.*) And this one's for Gary.
(*Sound of gunshot.*)

MIKAL: (*Tearing at his hair.*) Gary! What have you done!?

VOICE: (*Off.*) This one is for society.

GARY: (*Off.*) Yeah! It's as I planned it. Society gets the art it
deserves. Ha, ha, ha!
(*Sound of volley of gunshots.*
MIKAL tears at himself in the silence.)

Scene 5

Gary is a blank sheet on which society writes its horror story

GARY's jail cell.

NICOLE is with GARY, GARY is sitting on a chair. NICOLE is sitting astride him, facing him.

GARY: I love the vein on your forehead Nicole. Just as I love the one on your right tit. Didn't know I loved that one did yu? Ha, ha!
(*GARY opens her blouse.*)
You got no bra on.

NICOLE: I got no panties on either.

GARY: Jesus Christ, Nicole! I reckon we could do it! Now!

NICOLE: What about the screws?

GARY: Screw them!

NICOLE: You wouldn't, would you?
(*She giggles.*)

GARY: Maybe if they had a cute little ass like you got, baby. No, Christ! Course I wouldn't. But I could you. Now, why'd you think that is, eh? I can do it in here. For me, doing it in here is like other people doing it in a five star hotel. But doing it out there man is like doing it in jail. For me. That was my problem babe. If I coulda done it whenever I wanted to out there instead of being blasted on booze and uppers and downers I wouldn'ta done that murder. It's related see? Fucking is creative like painting; if you can't be creative you get destructive! (*Pause.*) You reckon I'm a jail bird?

NICOLE: Course not.

GARY: Yeah, well in the can I just can't get you outta my mind. I been jackin' off so much these last few weeks...
(*NICOLE kisses him.*)
...just thinking of you and the things we did.
(*She kisses him again.*)

I got to feeling like I was jackin' off too much, two,
three, four sometimes five times a day. Then they gave
me a little Fiorinal and that sleeper Dalmine at night.
The downers downed me and I didn't jack off so much
no more. And that always bothered me 'cos I never felt
like I really gave you a great wild sweating all controls
gone down to earth honest to gosh fuck.

(*NICOLE laughs outrageously.*)

I was just so hooked on that booze and Fiorinal and
I knew all the time that it was fucking me up sexually…
You, baby! My little bird who flew into my jail. My Life
jail! My paloma blanca!

(*They kiss.*)

Can you move onto it?

NICOLE: Yeah.

(*NICOLE moves to place herself on his penis.*
She settles.)

GARY: Jesus Christ Nicole!

NICOLE: Yeah!

GARY: You reckon you can keep it in?

NICOLE: Course I can keep it in!

(*She moves herself on GARY.*)

See?

GARY: No, Jesus! Ha, ha! I mean the noise! The noise of
your joy, baby!

NICOLE: O, Christ, Gary!

(*NICOLE laughs.*)

GARY: Sssh, ssh! Mmm, Mmmmm. O fuck! O fuck, baby!
This is too much! Too much!

NICOLE: Yeah, yeah! It is!

GARY: Stop! Stop! Don't move the slightest bit or I'll come.
Christ!

(*Silence.*
GARY's face is tight as he stops himself from coming.)

That's it!

NICOLE: You stop it?

GARY: Yeah.

NICOLE: How?

GARY: I just squeezed the top.

NICOLE: How could you have?

GARY: With my mind.

NICOLE: You squeezed your cock with your mind? What kind of mind is that Gary? Ha, ha!

GARY: It's the mind of a con! You learn to do a lot with your mind in here.

(*NICOLE laughs.*)

Let's talk.

NICOLE: Take our mind off it?

GARY: Yeah!

NICOLE: Okay. (*Pause.*) About what?

GARY: Okay. Listen. (*Pause.*) I gotta sell my body.

NICOLE: No, Gary! Don't talk about that. Talk about… Why don't you paint me? You could paint me in here. They'd give you the stuff.

GARY: Yeah. Sure, sure!

NICOLE: Paint each bit with care.

GARY: With total care. Make a separate painting of every hair on your pussy…

NICOLE: Yeah!

GARY: Your tits – each tit – especially the right one with the blue vein and your beautiful blue eyes, baby. And the beautiful little opening of your ass and put it on my ceiling so I could look up your ass every night before I go to sleep. And your lovely wet cunny, I'd paint that cunny crying for me and your clit yearning for my lick! But baby, see? I paint you every night. All the time.

(*They both suddenly cry out in orgasm together and bite their lips to suppress it while 'squirming' in the after-shock.*)

When they cut me up Nicole so I can sell the parts, you gotta get my dick.

NICOLE: Gary!

GARY: As I die I'll get a hard-on – it happens. An' I'll sure make sure they get instructions to tie that fucker off like a tourniquet so you get it full of my blood, my life blood baby!

(*NICOLE hangs onto GARY limply.*)

NICOLE: Don't Gary, don't.

(*Silence.*

NICOLE gets up. She pauses over GARY until he adjusts himself.

Silence.)

I gotta go.

GARY: Maybe I should leave my dick to the D.A. so he can go fuck himself. Or better, that salesman, so's he can go fuck himself for not letting me have the white truck when I wanted it which put me into such a fucking bad mood. That fucking truck! I fell in love with a fucking paint job!

NICOLE: Yeah Gary, I guess you did, I gotta go.

GARY: Nicole, Nicole! I know what you're thinking: Yeah I wouldn't paint you but I could fall in love with a paint job! I don't know, I'm so fucking screwed down baby!

NICOLE: You mean you're so fucking screwed up!

(*NICOLE goes.*)

GARY: Come and see me soon, Nicole!

(*As NICOLE leaves, she passes MIKAL coming on. There should be no recognition between the characters though this may be emphasised by some gesture from the actors.*)

Hey, Mikal! Who do you think I should leave my pecker to?

MIKAL: Why don't you give it to me?

GARY: You?

MIKAL: Yeah.

GARY: Why you?

MIKAL: So it can remind me what a prick you are.

GARY: Hey, hey, hey! I thought you'd want my eyes so's you could see the world artistically. Articulately.

MIKAL: I got your eyes, Gary.

GARY: What the fuck you mean by that?

MIKAL: I mean I'm seeing blue.

GARY: Christ! So what about my dick?

MIKAL: What is this?

GARY: You know me. The ladies man! What you think I'm a pessimist? You think I'm gonna let myself get chained to heaven in its entirety? You think I believe that shit?

You think it's all or nothing like that? You think dying's
gonna claim the whole works? Christ no, Mikey!
When I'm gone there's gonna be bits of me still working,
walking the streets, worrying the fuck out of this
worrisome fucking old world. And anyway, maybe I got
somebody I'd like you to use it on. So she don't ever
forget me. Na, fuck that. You lay off of her. Anyway, I got
correspondents: writing for this part of my body or that.

MIKAL: Sure, there's people who carry cards in their
wallets that say: 'if you find me dead you can have my
kidneys'. But that's not the same as knowing you're
gonna be gone on the seventeenth of January and
applicants are coming round now, one week before,
asking for your liver, your spleen, your left nut!
Christ man, it's sick.

(*GARY laughs.*)

It's cannibalism! Anyone else would cry out:
'For Christ's sake leave me in peace. I want my eyes!'
You know what you are Gary? Mediocrity enlarged by
history. They said that about Harry Truman. The only
thing he's remembered for is killing a million Japanese
with just two fucking bombs!

GARY: Is this you being the writer now?

(*GARY stands on his head in corner.*)

MIKAL: You gotta drop this shit Gary.

GARY: What shit?

MIKAL: Getting the state to top you. It scares the fuck
outta me. I don't know if I can live with it. Don't you
get me?

GARY: Get you? What you mean YOU!?

MIKAL: Get me! Get me! That's what I'm saying. Gary's
body's gonna fill my head. I can see it happening. I can
see it! I don't know how it's gonna happen or what's
gonna happen once it's happened but I know it's gonna
happen!

(*GARY stands on his feet.*)

GARY: Hey! You're dealing with a fucking historical
principal here! One that gives meaning to my life!
You don't get it? You don't get it! I can see it! See it in

YOUR eyes – which is the difference between us because
when I look I SEE. The whole fucking colossus of
conundrum! The whole fucking monster of enigma!
The whole fucking works!
(*As he speaks, GARY sits in a chair – the execution chair.*
He straps himself in and a hood is placed over his head.
He speaks through the hood.
Lights down.)

Scene 6

Gary is his own work of art

The same as Scene 4. GARY is in chair with a hood over his head.

GARY: Here's how it is kid! All my fucking life I been shit
in a drain! All my fucking life, what *I* mean's been
decided by the Meaners. The fuckers who make meaning
like Mama's fucking Dead Makers! So now I'm deciding!

MIKAL: Fuck you Gary! You're just a spoilt bastard!
You ever heard of cutting off your nose to spite your
face? You're a fucker Gary! I hate you! And I ain't gonna
come and fucking watch it!

GARY: You...

MIKAL: Fuck you!

GARY: I wouldn't give a fuck!

MIKAL: I won't be there!

GARY: Don't come! Don't come you shitty little runt, I'll be
better off without you!

MIKAL: Fuck you, Gary! Fuck you!

GARY: And that reminds me...

MIKAL: You fuck!

GARY: I gotta make a list. Of who I want in attendance.

MIKAL: You ain't just killing yourself Gary. That's the
fucking point! Fuck you!
(*MIKAL leaves.*
Somehow it should be contrived that GARY and his chair get
hoisted up so that by the time he gets shot he's as high as a roof.)

GARY: O, Mammy, Mammy! I don't wanna die! I don't
wanna die! Don't let them do it Mama! Ha, ha!

Fuck that! Listen: I got a duty as a member of this society that if anyone, ANYONE kills anyone else, they gotta kill that son of a bitch. That's what the rules says. If we don't follow the rules, why, we got nothing but articles of hypocrisy! Yeah! (*Pause.*) This is how I figure it Mikey! John Wayne is gonna die. Soon. He's got cancer. He's fading to nothing. John Wayne is not the man he was. And when he's dead he DEFINITELY won't be that man he was! But what does it mean? How about in two hundred years. Or two thousand years? Christ, no! He was a fucking actor! An actor who acted the killing of people. No questions asked. Well I raised a few questions! You say you're gonna kill me then you don't, why? Are you actors or killers? Am I just a member of the fucking audience? Am I just watching a film? Fuck you! You gotta do this killing! Then the circle is complete. Then I can understand. Then it means something! Old John Wayne, man. He just faded from the screen. Who can draw a story from this? John Wayne just faded man. No one got hurt. No one felt any pain. No one had Nicole chew their heart out. No one felt nothing! No one asked questions. That's the whole fucking point of John Wayne!

NICOLE: (*Voice off.*) Gary Gilmore! You hear me?

GARY: Yeah babe!

NICOLE: (*Voice off.*) Gary Gilmore, I love you!
   (*A volley of shots.*
   GARY slumps in his chair which now becomes the top of the Mormon Church.
   NICOLE comes on and begins stripping before the church.)

Scene 7

To love Gary is to hate authority

NICOLE is stripping outside church.

NICOLE: I'm out here you big heap of horse-shit church! Gary! When they kill you, one big balloon filled with all the air you ever breathed is gonna rise up above this

fucking church! Je love vous baby! Oh, Je love vous!
There must be a logic behind our destiny but I cannot
see even a particle of it...There are no longer words that
can express the love that is in my soul and my heart for
you mon Soul Mate! Remember how you sung 'Amazing
Grace' that time I took my clothes off outside the
fucking Mormon Church baby?!

> (*Sings.*) Amazing Grace that gave me you
> a fucking wretch like me!
> I once was lost in deepest blue
> now I swim with thee.

(*NICOLE repeats the verse over twice and GARY'S BODY
joins in.*)
You know what I'm thinking about now Gary? The way
you sit! The way you walked! The way you said things!
You have a danger Gary! Gary, you are one dangerous
fucker! Amazing Grace to you baby! Gary Gilmore one
dangerous fucker! You have a way of saying things!
You have a centre! We musta known each other from the
past. Musta! Did I ever tell you, Gary, how I was fucked
by my uncle when I was a little girl?
(*She sings her own 'Amazing Grace' again and again. GARY'S
BODY joins in.*)
I am often lost here and I will be that way often wherever
I am – till I feel your soul wrapped around me! Hold you
close and warm with your rough whiskery face in my
hands...take you to places I loved as a child, a dark little
glen in the forest of pines. It was my 'room'. So tightly
knit around with tall pine trees and forever-bearing
blackberry bushes. I used to lay in the middle of it on the
soft spring carpet of warm damp sweet-smelling pine
needles – gazing straight up from the walls of the trees –
up to a crystal blue sky and watch the cotton clouds sneak
by. Listen to my enchanted forest talking softly in its
thousand tongues.
(*She sings 'Amazing Grace' again.*)
Hey baby! I wrote you a song!

> (*Sings.*) For lost is my mind
> Silent by dawn

Loves away stolen
and hurting is long

So ask me no questions
sing me no song
follow me nowhere
I'm already gone.

(*NICOLE begins to go, collecting her clothes.*
She pauses to face the church then falls to her knees with her
arms in the air.)

Tell me church! Tell me God! Tell my soul: why do we
kill people who kill people to show that killing people is
wrong? Fucks!

(*Lights down.*)

Scene 8

To Bessie, Gary is the embodiment
of some inescapable, terrifying truth

BESSIE's trailer.

BESSIE: I'm out here on this verandah in Utah. The
verandah of my trailer. The stars are always in the
night. If they ever go out it'll make no difference.
To me. Everything is me. Gary is me. If Gary's dead
I'm a bit deader. Is there a place where we're not
trapped by this moment? If I walk into the room, the
step I just made is dead before I make the next one.
I want to be in heaven. In heaven, even the smallest
moment is big. The moment is the biggest thing.
This is what it comes down to. This is when we become
ourselves.

(*MIKAL comes on sniffing back tears.*)

MIKAL: Gary's dead.

(*Silence.*)

Just come over on the news.

BESSIE: Mikal, I lied! I saw the man hang! When I told
you I kept my head at my father's side so that I would
not see the execution? Just at the moment! Just at the

very moment when the trap-door was pulled, he pulled my head, my hair, yanked so hard to force me to watch the man as he dropped to his death! It was Gary! I was a little girl, Mikal, watching my son be executed. On the ride back I said I would NEVER, NEVER forgive my father and I would live my life to SPITE his hard virtue!

MIKAL: Jesus Christ Ma!

BESSIE: Gary was alive in SPITE of himself! He was dead before he was born! He's only gone back!

(*BESSIE holds her belly. She lets out a gasp and falls back onto the bed. She keeps hold of herself.*)

MIKAL: Ma!

BESSIE: It's alright son. The pains of bearing Gary. I'm having to bear them again.

MIKAL: Christ, I can't stand this! He's dead! They shot him!

(*BESSIE lets out a cry and holds tightly onto her belly.*)

BESSIE: (*Weaker.*) Listen! My life. My life has been a triumph of dark over light!

MIKAL: Ma! Stop it! Stop it! Or I don't know what I'm gonna do! I gotta get out of this shit!

BESSIE: You going to become a murderer Mikal?

MIKAL: No! No! I...I want to be. A writer.

(*BESSIE lets out a small cry of pain.*)

Ma, who's Nicole?

(*Silence. MIKAL goes. BESSIE lets out a cry. Blood comes from her mouth. She dies.*)

End of Part One.

PART TWO

Scene 1

Society is de-humanised. People are drowning in the darkness

MIKAL's bedsit. A bed, telephone, tape recorder/record player. There is an open suitcase. Scattered around are clothes, some letters etc.

(Music: Neil Young's song 'Pocahontas'.)

MIKAL looks rough – long, dirty hair.

He is naked, he is sitting on the bed. He is holding a bottle of whisky from which he's been drinking. Before him on a chair is propped a mirror.

He swigs from the bottle.

MIKAL: (*Laughing bitterly.*) Can't even get a hard-on to ja-ha-ha-hack myself off! Ha, ha!
(*He suddenly leaps up letting out a savage cry.*)
Pocahontas!
(*He pours some whisky down his front.*
He kicks the chair with the mirror on it. He falls back onto the bed.)
(*Phoney sobs.*) O, why? Why, my little willy? My little sharp-shooter! Tell 'em willy boy is here? Ha!
(*He puts a hand on his penis.*)
Nothing! Dead! Fucking dead!
(*He wraps the blanket around him. After a moment he sits up. He picks up the mirror and the chair and resets them.*)
(*Very serious.*) This is what I came to ask you Nicole, this is what I came to ask you: If Gary's murders are SIGNIFICANT and MEANINGFUL, they DESTROY meaning! Yeah? Why? Because those acts...those acts, then, say that murder has the power to end life in all its beauty – like the beauty of Nicole...

(*He swigs.*)

And IF his acts, these acts of murder are NOT powerful like this then what about the meaning of those two guys' lives? It's a heartbreaking conundrum little Nicole and I know you're gonna want to help me solve it because what do us you and I we people have left? Little baby Nicole, I've come down along this highway to find you...you. You Pocahontas. (*Suddenly wild.*) What about the Indians, man? What about the poor fucking shot, stabbed, ripped apart, gutted, EVISCERATED Indians? (*He swigs. GARY's face appears on the other side of the mirror. As MIKAL speaks, GARY'S BODY speaks exactly the same words in exactly the same way.*)

GARY'S BODY/MIKAL: (*Into the mirror.*) Why'm I talking like this? What does it mean? Am I talking like a writer! I've cleaned my own streets man but there's still fucking murders going on there! I killed fucking Indians, the Niggers, the Spicks and the Mexicans! But I am not killed! I am not killed! That's the fucking problem! I am NOT killed! I have not had my heart ripped out by State snipers; judgement men; apocalypse people! And I am dead without Pocahontas and without without without without without without without Nicole!
(*Silence.*)

MIKAL: She's the bullet in my brain! What must a woman like that be like? What kind of explosion happens in a man's head when he fucks her? Why am I talking about fucking her? I don't want to talk about fucking her! Look at you! Look at the face! Look at the face! Gilmore! What a fucking face! Christ! I hate you! Fucking hate you! Fucking, fucking, fucking, fucking hate you! C-u-u-u-uuuuuuuuuunt!!!!!!
(*Both fall from the mirror. MIKAL is in a state of collapse. He lays on the bed. GARY'S BODY comes around and sits on the other bed.*
Silence.)

GARY'S BODY: You're a writer. You get a phone.
(*Silence.*)

But don't fuckin' use it man.

MIKAL: Okay, Nicole, I came all the way down this
  highway.
  (*He picks up the phone.*)
GARY'S BODY: Shit! I don't believe this!
MIKAL: Across a whole fuckin' desert!
GARY'S BODY: Do not fuckin' believe it!
MIKAL: (*On the phone.*) Yeah. I'd...um... I'd...you got a
  number there for a Miss Nicole Barrett? (*Pause.*) Yeah.
  N. Barrett. (*Pause.*) A downtown number? I don't know.
  I don't have an address. Can you give me one? (*Pause.*)
  One-o-two-seven South Street? Yeah. That sounds like it
  could be it. Yeah. (*Pause.*)
  (*He writes down a number.*
  He puts down the phone.
  He takes a deep breath.)
  O fuck, man! O fuck!
GARY'S BODY: Don't do it you fuckin' grave robber!
MIKAL: O shit!
  (*He takes a deep breath and picks up the phone.*
  He puts down the phone again. He takes a swig from bottle.
  He picks up the phone again.)
GARY'S BODY: It'd be necrophilia man! She's with me in
  heaven!
  (*MIKAL dials. He listens.*)
MIKAL: Hello. (*Pause.*) O...u... I'm u... Nicole? Nicole
  Barrett? (*Pause.*) Norman? Okay. Sorry, wrong number.
GARY'S BODY: Ha, ha! Norman! You fuckin' jerk off!
  (*MIKAL picks up phone.*)
MIKAL: I'm looking for a Barrett. (*Pause.*) Yeah, Nicole
  Barrett. N. Barrett. (*Pause.*) No, it's okay I tried that.
  Thanks.
  (*He puts the phone down. He gets up. He paces a little.*
  GARY's BODY watches him with a joyous grin.
  Suddenly, MIKAL stops. He's thought of something.)
  Jesus!
  (*He sits and picks up the phone.*)
  I want a number. (*Pause.*) Yeah. L.A. Yeah it's for a Miss
  Nicole – N for Norman – Nicole Gilmore. Yeah. What?
  As in Gary? Yeah, Jesus! Yeah. Nicole Gilmore. As in
  Gary Gilmore.

(*GARY'S BODY looks expectant almost with horror.*)
You do?
(*GARY'S BODY bites his fist.*)
Okay. Thank you.
(*MIKAL writes down number. He dials. GARY'S BODY continues to bite his fist.*)
Hello. (*Pause.*) Hello. Is that...? Is that Nicole? (*Pause.*) Barrett? (*Pause.*) Gary's brother. Mikal. (*Pause.*) Hiya, Nicole. No, we never met.
(*GARY'S BODY curls into a ball crying out.*)
GARY'S BODY: Gilmore! Nicole fuckin' Gilmore!
(*Lights down.*)

Scene 2

What makes a man charismatic?

The same.

MIKAL is wearing shirt and trousers. He's trying to look decent. He is sitting on the bed drinking. There is a knock on the door. He puts the bottle down.

NICOLE comes on.

NICOLE: Hiya, I'm Nicole.
(*Silence.*
MIKAL looks at NICOLE with wonder.
She comes in.
Silence.)
MIKAL: Sure is a nice day.
NICOLE: Yeh. Sun must be shining all the way to Sacramento. You know how warm it is?
MIKAL: No. (*Pause.*) I got no thermometer.
(*Silence.*)
NICOLE: O.
(*She laughs.*)
MIKAL: What?
NICOLE: You wouldn't carry a thermometer around, would you?
(*MIKAL chuckles.*)

MIKAL: D'you want to smoke some dope?

NICOLE: No thanks. (*Pause.*) How did you get my number?

MIKAL: I checked with the operator.

NICOLE: That easy?

MIKAL: Yeah. You made it easy. Using Gary's name.

NICOLE: Yeah. I guess that's right.

You can kiss me if you want.

(*MIKAL looks surprised.*)

It's okay. (*Pause.*) First time I kissed Gary is something
I remember. Gary bought a six-pack. He put the six-pack
on my knee. I said, it hurt. Joking. Then he rubbed my
knee. He did it decently. It felt good in a nice simple
way. Then he asked me if he could kiss me. (*Pause.*)

(*Silence.*

*MIKAL kisses NICOLE tentatively. She takes his head in
her hands and kisses him fully. She takes off whatever her top
is, revealing her nakedness. GARY'S BODY comes on.
He circles them looking appalled. NICOLE takes off MIKAL's
shirt. She kisses him and helps him onto the bed. MIKAL
looks bewildered.*

GARY'S BODY gets onto the other bed.

*NICOLE lays on the bed and MIKAL gets on top of her and
begins pumping away.*

NICOLE speaks to the audience as MIKAL pumps.

*During the following scene, GARY'S BODY responds in a
variety of ways: cowering, outraged, with hands over eyes,
pathetically sad etc.*)

(*To the audience.*) So here I was again. Only now with the
brother. And he's pumping away but he's drunk too
much and can't get a hard on. Why doesn't he stop and
rest? He'll just keep going till he's whacked out and
looks like he's been hit with a tyre lever! After a while
he'll say…

MIKAL: You gotta help me Nicole.

NICOLE: (*To the audience.*) I know me. I'll always do what I
can to bring a half decent fuck out of one of these
sad boys.

(*They turn over and NICOLE puts her head between MIKAL's
legs and moves back and forth.*)

(*To the audience.*) But my neck just got so tired…

(*MIKAL then looks up and talks to the audience.*)

MIKAL: (*To the audience.*) Then she says…

NICOLE: (*To MIKAL.*) Let's just cool it for a while. (*To the audience.*) Then he said:

MIKAL: (*To NICOLE.*) Well anyway, I don't want to fuck you I want to make love to you.

NICOLE: (*To the audience.*) And I says… (*To MIKAL, slightly cynical.*) Yeah. I know. (*To the audience.*) And within, what, a minute? he's saying…

MIKAL: Get on top of me. (*To the audience.*) I asked her gently!

NICOLE: (*To the audience.*) He did.

(*NICOLE gets on top of MIKAL and moves.*)

(*To the audience.*) I'm trying but it's no good and he says…

MIKAL: It's the booze, baby. The booze, the speed and the dope – which I gotta take to stop going mad!

NICOLE: (*To the audience.*) I just had the feeling that it would always be like this. In the end it just made me so mad!

(*MIKAL gets out of the bed angrily pulling his trousers up.*)

MIKAL: I can't make it! You know why!

(*MIKAL swigs from the whisky bottle.*)

NICOLE: (*Morosely.*) 'Cos you're drinking too much.

GARY'S BODY: Because you're not her fucking lover man!

MIKAL: No! It's in here. (*Pointing to his chest.*) In here deep!

(*MIKAL sits on bed.*)

I've been having this dream. About the house where I grew up. In the dream it's always night. It's my father's house. On the outskirts of town. A dead-end American town. A train whistle blows out in the night but no train ever comes.

GARY'S BODY: What is this shit? Writer!

(*GARY'S BODY makes a masturbatory gesture.*)

MIKAL: People go from the darkness outside the house to the darkness inside. Everybody's back from the dead. My mother, Bessie, my young brother Galen who got knifed and died in the arms of his young fucking wife and Gary who killed those guys in a total fuckin' rage against the way he'd been robbed by life.

NICOLE: He killed those guys 'cos he couldn't fuck me!

GARY'S BODY: Right on babe! Tell it as it is!

MIKAL: (*Horrified.*) How can you say that!? They died because he couldn't fuck you?

NICOLE: Yeah! And for all I know you'll do the same!

GARY'S BODY: Ho, ho! Fucking hit it!

NICOLE: (*Angry.*) What do you think he was? Some kind of tortured fucking angel?

MIKAL: He was an artist!

NICOLE: Yeah! I know!

MIKAL: I know! And he didn't think it had any worth! His own art!

NICOLE: What're you saying?

MIKAL: I'm saying if you don't believe in your own art, what DO you believe in? You gotta have a stake in things to believe. The link was missing. It wasn't put there. Gary ripped up his painting in front of me! You were like his best painting. But it's like he wasn't allowed to have you. Like it was decreed!

NICOLE: And that's why he killed those guys?

MIKAL: Yeah! 'cos when art's got no worth, the artist becomes a killer.

NICOLE: That's shit! Gary had a picture of his life: ABCD. A: In seventh grade his class voted on whether to send valentines to one another. He was the only kid who voted against it. So he bought valentines to mail to everybody. But no one sent him one. B: One night he broke the window of the gunstore with a brick. He cut his hand but he got the gun he wanted. A Winchester semi-automatic. Later he got some shells and went plinking. Fucking plinking! But he got tired of hiding the gun from his old man so he threw it in the creek. He didn't want it if he couldn't have it just the way he wanted it. C: On his thirteenth birthday his mother said he could pick between having a party or getting a twenty dollar bill. He chose the party and invited just two kids.

They spent the money they'd been given for Gary's presents on theirselves. And they told him. D: He had a fight with one of the kids whose dad told him off. Told him to stay away. Soon after that, Gary got into trouble for something else and got sent to Reform School. Because if he couldn't have it the way he wanted it someone had to pay! He ripped those paintings up in front of you 'cos he couldn't have his painting the way he wanted. Just like he couldn't have me the way he wanted! That's America, man! The AMER-ican fuckin' Dream!

(*Silence.*)

MIKAL: Last night I dreamed it again. I'm left sitting in the living room. Gary comes in and says:

GARY'S BODY: Mikal, you can never join the family in its comings in and goings out. Because you have not yet entered death. You cannot follow us across the tracks, into the forest where our real lives take place, until you die.

MIKAL: He pulls a gun out.

(*GARY'S BODY produces a gun.*)

He lays it on my lap.

(*GARY'S BODY places the gun on MIKAL's lap.*)

There's a door across the room and he moves towards it.

(*GARY'S BODY moves towards the door.*)

Through the door is the night. I can see the glimmer of the tracks. Beyond them, my family.

(*MIKAL suddenly jumps up.*)

(*Feverishly.*) I don't hesitate! I pick up the pistol! I put its barrel into my mouth. I pull the trigger.

(*Sound of gun shot, MIKAL falls, NICOLE screams.*)

NICOLE: No!

GARY'S BODY: (*At the door.*) He feels the back of his head erupt.

(*NICOLE cradles MIKAL's head in her lap. She is sobbing.*)

MIKAL: (*Dazed.*) It's a softer feeling than I expected!

GARY'S BODY: He would have felt his teeth fracture, disintegrate and pass in a gush of blood out of his mouth.

MIKAL: I feel my life pass out of my mouth and in that instant, I collapse into nothingness.

(*NICOLE cuddles MIKAL's head and rocks back and forth gently.*)

NICOLE: O, God! Mikal! Gary, Mikal!

(*Lights down.*)

Scene 3

Dead men can't come

The same, later.

MIKAL and NICOLE are asleep in separate beds.

GARY'S BODY is sitting on NICOLE's bed. He gets up. He gently pulls the bedclothes back. He delicately puts her legs apart. She groans. He gets on top of her as though he were making love. There is no reaction from her.

After a moment NICOLE gasps. GARY'S BODY stops. NICOLE's eyes open. She is looking at GARY'S BODY but not seeing him.

GARY'S BODY returns to sitting on the edge of the bed.

He is crying.

GARY'S BODY: O, God! To look into those eyes! I'm sorry baby! I couldn't do it. I'm dead!
(*NICOLE suddenly gets up. She goes to MIKAL and kneels beside his bed. She puts an arm around him. He stirs. GARY'S BODY lays in NICOLE's bed making a point of laying in the shape she's left.*)

When murder is charismatic, art has malfunctioned

NICOLE: Mikal!
(*She shakes him.
MIKAL is awake.
Silence.*)
NICOLE: Mikal! It doesn't matter that you couldn't do it.
MIKAL: (*Weepily.*) I feel so miserable.
NICOLE: You got a hangover. You've been asleep.
MIKAL: No! You don't understand. I didn't want to do it.

49

NICOLE: You didn't?

MIKAL: No.

NICOLE: You got a funny way of showing it!
(*She laughs.*)
I been dancing with your pissed-limp dick for four hours!
(*She laughs.*
Silence.)

MIKAL: I want to write...something. I need to understand. I feel so screwed up!
(*NICOLE begins to dress.*)

NICOLE: I gotta go. It's getting late.

MIKAL: (*Taking hold of her.*) I've got to have answers.

NICOLE: There's no answers. It's just streets full of cops.
(*She pulls herself free.*)

MIKAL: (*Horrified.*) That's all?
(*NICOLE continues to dress.*)

NICOLE: God's in his heaven and the cops are on the street. I know what you're into. You want to know the meaning of why it all happened. Who's going to tell you? Some philosopher? I'm not. God's in his heaven and the cops are on the street. But why is God in his heaven? Because people fuck! If people didn't fuck there wouldn't be no people and if there were no people there'd be no God; or if there was He'd be redundant and man that would be diminishing! I'm waiting for the day when I can compare a good, honest, no-holds-barred fuck with a home!
(*Silence.*)

MIKAL: (*Bitterly.*) So what about Roger Eaton?

NICOLE: Who?

MIKAL: Roger fucking Eaton! All the Roger Eatons! All the nice clean guys?

NICOLE: Roger Eaton?

MIKAL: Yeah! Fucking Roger!

NICOLE: Jesus! What?... How d'you know about Roger Eaton?

MIKAL: Who doesn't? This is what really fucks me and Gary up! The Roger Eatons! The Mr Clean who never

wears a dirty shirt, who's always shaved, combed hair, who you never see take a shit, who never as far as you know ever takes a shit! You go for a dude like that and who are we? Yeah. That's who fucks us up: the Mr Cleans. Mr Hi baby, I'll be home at five, fix me a Manhattan and we'll take in a show – there's a play at the Arts should be good – then dinner and hey baby ain't life fucking great and when we get home a night-cap and a nice clean fuck – scented fuck after, of course, we've taken a bath together and maybe fucked in there too…how do you think I can live with Roger Eaton fucking you in my brain? And don't you know that these are the very dudes who screw up everything else too? Who take possession of the Art world so that Gary's left outside and his work becomes worthless and when his art becomes worthless murder becomes charismatic! Roger Eaton worming away at the core who fucked in public right there in the newspapers! Not to mention all the other fucks you fucked while Gary was in the can struggling with his destiny like a Greek fucking warrior, a destiny that you and Mr Roger fucking Eaton imposed.
(*NICOLE gets up.*)

NICOLE: Shut up! Shut up! I've had enough of you fucking messed up Mormon Gilmores!
(*MIKAL swipes NICOLE across the face.*
GARY'S BODY jumps up. NICOLE falls back. GARY'S BODY holds her face.
Silence.)
(*Crying.*) It's your gods who fucked you up. And your fucking prophets. I've known so many of you guys, all been like kids who don't know what to do: scared of God. Don't you think that's why Gary killed them guys? To get God's attention? And when he asked for his own execution well hell, God's got to pay some time to him then because he's going to have to decide what to do with old Gary Gilmore. Well that's a real fuck-up for me because I don't know how to deal with philosophers! You, Gary and the cops, you're all the same. You are the mess that's doing me in!

(*GARY'S BODY sits back down on the bed and listens to the
story with deep interest.*
She uses the mirror to put some make-up on.)
Like one day my little Jeremy is on the grass of
somebody's lawn naked, 'cos I'd let the kids play like
that when I had no money for diapers or even laundry
soap to clean the dirty ones – even though Gary
always had his six-pack...
(*MIKAL aggressively pops a pill and swallows it with a swig
from the bottle.*)

MIKAL: How can I be a writer if I can't fuck?

NICOLE: It doesn't matter!

MIKAL: How do you know it doesn't matter?

NICOLE: What did you take then?

MIKAL: Some speed.

NICOLE: Speed! And there you fucks go round and round
with your blue lights flashing.
(*Sound of police sirens.*)

NICOLE: And all the other kids are playing in this ditch
but Jeremy's on the lawn and suddenly...
(*Sound of police siren again.*)
You could believe that! Somebody's called the cops and
this fat cop drives right up to my house and starts laying
down this unbelievable shit...

VOICE OF COP: You know, lady, your kids are in danger
of their lives playing in the ditch down there.
(*MIKAL looks afraid.*)

NICOLE: This is what he said! And I said (*Shouting to off.*)
they're not in danger of their lives, they're in danger of
YOURS!

VOICE OF COP: Your little boy could drown.

NICOLE: You see: he's gone from my KIDS to my little
boy which he's singled out because he's nude. I said
(*Shouting to off.*) Mister! You don't know what you're
talking about! My little boy wasn't anywhere near that
water. He doesn't have one drop on his body, which, if
you'll let your perverted eyes look at, you'll see.

VOICE OF COP: Okay! But I got phone calls from the
neighbours about you're not taking proper care of
your kids!

NICOLE: (*To MIKAL.*) It's out there. The voice! It's in the
mists about Utah. And I said: (*Shouting to off.*) Get off
my property! Get your fucking ass down the road!

VOICE OF COP: Hey you watch it lady 'cos all I gotta do
is file one report and you lost those kids, okay? I got the
welfare people right here. Right here at the end of this
telephone line!

NICOLE: (*To off.*) Go fuck yourself! And I slammed
the door.
(*Loud slam.*)

VOICE OF COP: I better not see those kids outside! Got it?

NICOLE: (*Screaming to off.*) Those kids are going to play
outside all the god-damned day, and you better not touch
them, or I'll shoot you!
(*Silence.*)
The cop just stood there; didn't know what to do.
He drives off. (*Pause.*) That did my fucking head in!
I've always done the best for my fucking kids and that
son-of-a-bitch cop... He may as well have there and then
come in and tore out every last bit of fuck I had in me.
And instead?... I forgot. Gary's still in bed and, in those
days the bed had to be moved right up to the window
'cos of the hot nights. And now it's different: it's not me
that was hurt, put down, insulted, but Gary. His head's
done in because he's got this trunk-full of guns and I'd
forgotten he was there and I'm shouting like that at the
cop and he could have busted us right there and then.
But I gotta live on this street and I got rights! Only
those rights are different from Gary's and he just...
(*GARY'S BODY gets up from the bed. He starts walloping
NICOLE about the head.*)
...lay the fuck right into me...
(*GARY'S BODY hits NICOLE all round the room.*)

GARY'S BODY: What? You stuck your brain up your ass?
All I got is to stay asleep and that pig-fucker is in here
picks me up on suspicion searching my room and he's
got my guns and I'm back in the slammer and you don't
get no slammer, no red-hot Gilmore poker up your
yearning butt, baby!

53

NICOLE: …beating the shit out of me.
>*(MIKAL covers his head not wanting to see or hear.)*

O, no! It's not me that's insulted and hurting, it's Gary!
GARY'S BODY: You got too big a mouth!
NICOLE: Always fuckin' Gary! And I just wanted to protect the freedom of my little kids in this country of freedom!
>*(GARY'S BODY returns to his bed like a big guy.*
>*Pause.)*

You people – Gilmores and cops, you're all the same.
I gotta go. I gotta see my kids.
>*(NICOLE begins to go. MIKAL stops her.)*

MIKAL: I can't let you go.
NICOLE: What!
MIKAL: You're not going. I'm locking the door. You go and I'll fucking kill somebody or I'll kill myself!
NICOLE: Why?
MIKAL: I don't know.
>*(Pause.)*

NICOLE: *(Bitterly.)* See? You're all the same.
>*(Silence.*
>*They become locked in their poses.)*

GARY'S BODY: I knew I should've taken you with me baby. I just knew it! O, baby, I know what he's doing! I just know it!

If there was a heaven, we'd have to go through hell to get there; most people settle for hell

MIKAL suddenly jumps up and hits NICOLE so hard that she falls onto the bed into the arms of GARY'S BODY. GARY'S BODY cradles her, fondling her face and hair. He is crying.

NICOLE is sobbing.

MIKAL: *(Crazed.)* You know most people in this life settle for hell! Why've you got to be different?
NICOLE: I don't know what you mean!
MIKAL: You don't know?
NICOLE: No!

MIKAL: No reincarnation! No coming back! No karma shit!
Gary's dead and you need hell 'cos it's easier! Settle for
what you're given. Gary did.

GARY'S BODY: This is my fault. I brought you into
this baby.

(*MIKAL picks NICOLE up roughly and throws her onto his
own bed.*)

MIKAL: And I'm settling for it too!

(*MIKAL sits astride NICOLE.*)

You think I'm going to waste my time writing in a world
that's never going to listen to me? That's so fucked up?
I'm just not gonna bother!

(*MIKAL slaps NICOLE. She tries to fight back.*)

NICOLE: Fuck off! Get off me!

(*GARY'S BODY tries to pull MIKAL off. But nothing
happens.*)

MIKAL: Well maybe I should fucking kill you!

GARY'S BODY: I can't do anything! I'm fuckin' powerless,
man!

(*MIKAL lifts his hand to hit NICOLE.*)

(*Tearfully.*) Fuck this! Yes, definitely fuck this!

(*He turns his back on them, and gets onto his bed, on his
elbow and knees, burying his head in the pillow.*)

NICOLE: Go on! Go on you cheap fuck! You fucking pale
imitation! See if you can do it! I loved Gary for killing
those two guys. Don't you just know that? He became
my fucking hero!

(*GARY puts his hands over his ears.*
MIKAL begins to throttle NICOLE.)

MIKAL: I'm going to be fucking free!

(*After a moment he suddenly stops. He gets up. He's half-
crying.*
NICOLE is coughing etc.)

I gotta go out. Don't try and leave!

(*MIKAL goes.*
NICOLE sits on bed rocking back and forth, sobbing.
GARY'S BODY gets up and out of his bed.
He stands in front of her as if he wants to show off his body.
He pauses.)

GARY'S BODY: Ain't sex a bitch baby? When it's going well you're right on top of it so it seems of only small importance and you wonder what the fuss was all about when you weren't getting it. But when it's not going well it's right on top of you and it's making you feel small. And you wonder with all your health and strength and with all your life what can you do to get it? And then, of course, when you get it you're resentful of the struggle it took to get it! You're thinking: maybe it's not enough. (*Pause.*) That's why I wanted to fuck your little sister. She was in the truck the night I shot the first guy. She was the reason I did it. Not because I wasn't having sex with you but because I couldn't have sex with her. Your little sister. It wouldn't have been right: me, Gary Gilmore, I was thirty-six she's fourteen. In the world we lived in it wouldn't be right so I had to change the world. The way I changed the world was killing that first guy. Then the world was changed: into my image. Which meant I made the rules. Which meant I could then, if I wanted, fuck your little sister. She must've run off when she heard the gun shot. I don't know but that's my excuse baby!

(*MIKAL comes on with a bottle. He sits, opens it and drinks deeply.*
Silence.)

NICOLE: Did you ever hear Gary's tape?

(*GARY'S BODY goes back to his bed.*)

MIKAL: What tape?

NICOLE: Utah Blue.

GARY'S BODY: Don't play it, Nicole! It was just for you!

MIKAL: (*Aggressively.*) I've never heard of it! What is it?

NICOLE: It's a tape Gary made. Just before they killed him.

(*MIKAL looks bewildered.*)

It's his last thoughts!

MIKAL: I don't believe you!

NICOLE: I'll go and get it.

MIKAL: Huh! And you won't come back.

NICOLE: If I wouldn't come back you may as well kill me now. But if I don't go you'll never know if there was a tape.

(In the 'lights down' there is the sound of footsteps running as if down endless corridors in a nightmare.

In the darkness, MIKAL smashes the bottle and cuts his wrists with it, letting out a cry.)

Scene 4

Nicole helps Mikal survive pessimism to struggle against his culture

The same.

MIKAL is laying on the floor. NICOLE is bent over him bandaging his wrist. GARY'S BODY is laying on bed propped on his arm – as he may have been when he and MIKAL were young: interested in listening to something.

GARY'S BODY gets up a little, surprised when NICOLE comes on.

NICOLE: You crazy bastard! I said I was coming back!

GARY'S BODY: Joseph Smith, Brigham Young, those Mormons had to be self-obsessed sons of bitches. Nicole flew in like a dove with a message of beauty and just got fucked around in the shit of all of us. You could never touch her Mikal. She is a fuckin' poem. But you know that; that's why you slit your wrists! Lucky my fucking angel of mercy came back to save you. On your road to Calvary. And you tried to fucking strangle her!

NICOLE: You're lucky it's not much. More like a cry for help than the end of a writer. You missed the artery; hit a vein, that's all.

MIKAL: (*Weakly.*) I suppose Gary hit arteries.

(*Silence as NICOLE finishes the bandaging. She helps MIKAL up and sits him in the chair. She takes out the tape and holds it up to show him. She puts the tape in the machine*

*but doesn't switch it on. She approaches MIKAL (who is
totally unprepared for affection). She strokes his head etc.
and eventually sits astride him. She begins moving very
carefully and gently on MIKAL. MIKAL looks at her with
wonder. GARY'S BODY now sits up. She continues to move,
then stops.)*

NICOLE: You're ready.

*(MIKAL continues to look at NICOLE with wonder. NICOLE
gets up from MIKAL and switches on the tape. She returns to
MIKAL. She sits astride him. She motions this: she takes
MIKAL's penis (out of his trousers.) and, very carefully, with
great purpose, puts it inside her. Both have held breath. While
the tape plays, they fuck – first slowly then more and more
energetically. They both come as GARY'S VOICE says: 'I love
you baby. From out here in the blue'.)*

GARY'S VOICE: (*On tape.*) This tape I made for you
Nicole, I call Utah Blue. Why not? I'm a fucking artist
ain't I? It's my blue period. Utah. Trouble is it's been my
whole fucking life. (*Pause.*) People're going to want to
know why I killed those two boys. They done nothing to
me; there was no reason to do it to them. But I did it
cold and I did it with a certain kind of humour. Hell one
of those guys gave me a big smile just as I blew his head
apart! But, you know, I was just actin'; just playing a part
because you know, baby, deep in me is BLUE. It's as
though I've lived many times before and each time I've
caused women to cry and babies to become orphans.
And the thought of that, the thought of that BLUE
always makes me so scared I have to go and do
something that'll kill the scaredness. And I can prove
that this is true. I can prove that I killed those two guys
to try and wash away all that Utah Blue. 'Cos I killed the
second guy a whole day after I killed the first! That's the
proof! 'Cos when I killed the first guy I killed the fear
but then, during the whole next day, things got bluer
than ever. Things got bluer than ever things were before
and I kind of lost control and I got real scared then 'cos
I'd killed that first guy and so the only way I could get

over the killing, the killing of the first guy, was to go out
and kill the second one! (*Suddenly angry.*) And if I hadn't
shot my fucking thumb off I probably would have gone
out and shot a whole lot of other guys because that's the
nature, baby, of livin' in the substance. Living in Utah
Blue. Blue is murder and murder and murder. Blue is
what I lived with in my earlier lives and it's what I lived
with from the moment I come into this one, which is
why I'm taking steps to beat the karma rap in advance of
the next one baby. It's Spinoza. It's all part of the one
substance. There's no way out. You can just amend
things. And listen baby! Don't you go fuckin' that Roger
Eaton when I'm gone, nor none of them horny biker
fucks you said you met. I love you baby. From out here
in the blue.

(*The tape runs blank.*
Silence.
During the fuck, GARY'S BODY paces, looks closely, turns
away, pulls at himself, is horrified etc. When they and the
tape finish, they hang onto each other limply, in silence.
In the silence, GARY'S BODY, crying, sits astride MIKAL's
knees with his arms around NICOLE. He holds her tight
while speaking into her ear.)

GARY'S BODY: Blue is one fuck of a colour babe. It's way
out there as far as you can go to that flying place your
fuck could take me, – O Jesus, you knew how to take the
fuck way out to supersede ordinary understanding to
meaning itself – and blue is also the sadness in my heart
that I could only ever fuck you in jail. I jacked off a lot in
jail 'cos I couldn't have you. Dreaming about you.
About doing it with you. Isn't that a blue sad thing?
But I couldn't handle the streets of Utah! With their blue
lights flashin' and cops in blue suits and the blues.
I always get the blues. (*Pause.*) I'm jacking off even more
these days. In heaven. Maybe ten times a day.

(*MIKAL lets out a full, carefree, wild, happy, laugh.*)

NICOLE: (*With laughter in her voice.*) What?

MIKAL: Nothing. Just a thought came to my mind.

NICOLE: What?

MIKAL: I could just imagine Gary in heaven. He wouldn't give a fuck!

(*They both laugh loudly.*

GARY'S BODY holds onto NICOLE tighter.

NICOLE and MIKAL kiss as GARY'S BODY speaks.)

GARY'S BODY: (*Crying.*) Why couldn't my Utah Blue be no more, no more, no more evil and definitely no more beautiful than lickin' Nicole's pussy out before that congregation of Dead Makers? Or buggering her on the altar of Mormon! O, Christ! Baby! Could I make it blue with you! I would fuck you till the cows come home in every big and little hole from your pussy to your ass hole to your ear hole and never not once more ever in any life I ever had ever never want again to even ever touch another person in anger let alone kill one!

(*NICOLE gets up from MIKAL as though GARY'S BODY weren't there.*)

NICOLE: You can write now.

(*They look at each other in silence.*

NICOLE leaves. MIKAL looks after her blissfully.

MIKAL gets up, helping GARY'S BODY off as if he were merely a shadow.

MIKAL is very upbeat. He gets himself together, packing things up etc.)

MIKAL: (*Lightly.*) Gary?

GARY'S BODY: (*Surprised.*) Mikey?

MIKAL: There was no meaning in it was there?

GARY'S BODY: Meaning?

MIKAL: In your fight to be executed. As though it was some search for meaning.

GARY'S BODY: (*Defiantly.*) What do you mean?

MIKAL: That if society didn't carry out its own BELIEFS and kill you then there's no meaning in anything.

GARY'S BODY: That's it. Yeah.

MIKAL: But what kind of meaning is it, man, that you gotta kill two guys to get near it!

GARY'S BODY: It's my meaning! Gary Gilmore's fucking meaning!

(*MIKAL stops what he's doing.*)

MIKAL: Yeah, that's right! And d'you know what? It's making fucking Mormons of us all! Don't you think that's ironic?

(*Silence.*)

(*Placidly.*) Just tell me Gary that you killed those guys because you were in a bad mood. Something like that. Because if you don't, if you keep trying to put some meaning on it then…then what have I got? I'm dead! I may as well be dead! There'd be no point in going on. You gotta tell me that you killed those guys 'cos you couldn't get the white truck and you couldn't get Nicole back!

(*Silence.*)

You gotta do this for me!

(*Silence.*)

(*Suddenly angry.*) Jesus Christ! I gotta live my life! How'm I going to do it if I gotta believe that you whom I love, LOVED so DEEPLY, murdered for the greatest love, murdered okay because jail had taken away your familiarity with fucking but nevertheless murdered in the name of the greatest expression of love. How'm I going to do it? Release me Gary! Just fucking release me! Just say that it is so and it is so!

GARY'S BODY: Say WHAT is so?

MIKAL: Say that there was no meaning in it! Just say: killing the two guys was meaningless and your own death was meaningless. A meaningless act. In fact, an act of MURDER! That you got the state to help you commit suicide. Say it!

GARY'S BODY: What about me, then? I gotta freeze out here with my broken karma?

MIKAL: Gary! It's you or me! You freeze out there or burn in here! Just say it! Say it is so! And IT WILL BE SO!

(*Silence.*)

Gary?

GARY'S BODY: What?

MIKAL: Say it! Say it is so!

GARY: Say it is so?

MIKAL: Yes.

GARY: Christ, that's nothing! It is so! What's the big deal?
It is so. It is so. Who gives a fuck?
(*GARY'S BODY goes.*
Silence. After a few moments, MIKAL bursts into a full laughter.
Lights go down to Neil Young singing 'Pocahontas'.)

The End.

OVER MILK WOOD

for Hazel Walford Davies

Characters

HUW PUGH

SINEAD

MRS PUGH

GLADYS

LITTLE OLD LADY

JACK

TONY

ROGER

VOICE OF DYLAN'S GHOST

Over Milk Wood was first presented by the Spectacle Theatre Co. at Porth Comprehensive School, on 27 October 1999; it moved to the Theatr Felinfach, on 8 November 1999, and then continued on a tour of Wales, with the following cast:

HUW PUGH, Owen Garmon

SINEAD, Karen Wynne

MRS PUGH/GLADYS/
LITTLE OLD LADY/
JACK/TONY/ROGER, Rhodri Evans

VOICE OF DYLAN'S GHOST (on tape), Owen Garmon

Director, Steve Davis

Designer, Terry Chinn

Stage Management, George Davis-Stewart

Music, Pete Stacey

The Company

Artistic Director, Steve Davis

Administrative Director, Sandra Jones

Company Stage Manager, George Davis-Stewart

Assistant Administrator, Michelle Collins

Administration Assistant, Elaine Lord

Notes

1.   The 'soundtrack' may be a cacophony of voices speaking a jumble of lines from the original play *Under Milk Wood*. This could be played as music. In the text it will be referred to as The Voices.

2.   The central feature of the set is a stairs. But rather than these being a long multi-stepped staircase it would be better if they were three or four very large steps (made from, say, three or four rostra) put together with a large area at the top that may, where necessary, be in shadow.

Scene 1

The home of Mr & Mrs Huw Pugh
25 January 1954

HUW comes on carrying a large 1950s wireless. He's walking on tiptoe.

What we see of MRS PUGH is little more than a large shape in the shadow at the top of the stairs.

She is snoring.

HUW: (*Sotto voce to the audience.*) The wife is in bed. Said she had a headache. It's gas. She accumulates the kind of gases that a sperm whale accumulates and lets out through that hole in its head. Only, she hasn't got a hole in her head. (*Pause. Cheekily.*) Well not yet anyway! (*Giggles quietly.*) No. I've had to borrow this wireless because there's something I want to listen to tonight and she won't have one in the house. (*Pause.*) Marriage! It's frightening. When I married her she was eight stone with golden hair and lemon skin and eyes full of shooting stars. Now she looks like Winston Churchill! If Winston Churchill had been of her sex he would not have been the kind of woman I would have chosen to be my wife!

MRS PUGH: (*Voice off.*) HUW!
(*HUW sighs.*)

MRS PUGH: (*Voice off.*) What are you doing?

HUW: Um…nothing. Mam.

MRS PUGH: (*Voice off.*) You cretin! Nothing is the opposite of doing! How can you be doing nothing? You're so indecisive! Never knowing who you are or where you're going!

HUW: Alright then. I'm not doing nothing.

MRS PUGH: (*Voice off.*) So then you are doing SOMEthing! (*HUW is fiddling with dial on radio.*)

HUW: (*To the audience.*) SHE should be the teacher, not me. She's a philosopher. I am the insect of her deliberations. We all know it's the ant's lot to be crushed.

MRS PUGH: (*Voice off.*) What are you mumbling? You see? MUMBLING! This is why you've never mounted to anything!

HUW: (*To the audience.*) I've mounted a few things! (*To MRS PUGH.*) I'm not mumbling! I'm practising my Welsh. *Yr wyf i, yr wyt ti, y mae hef, y mae hi...*

MRS PUGH: (*Voice off.*) There's not much point in that! There's no one within these four walls who'd understand you!

(*Sound of air waves coming from the radio.*)

MRS PUGH: (*Voice off.*) What's that?

HUW: A wireless.

MRS PUGH: (*Voice off.*) Here?

HUW: Yes.

MRS PUGH: (*Voice off.*) You'd better explain yourself!

HUW: I want to listen to something.

MRS PUGH: (*Voice off.*) Not in this house you're not!

HUW: But it's here now!

MRS PUGH: (*Voice off.*) I won't have it! The next thing, you'll be bringing home women!

HUW: It's Dylan's play.

MRS PUGH: (*Voice off.*) Dylan's dead! And deserves to be. He's turned half the men of this village into alcoholics!

HUW: No! They were all determined drinkers!

MRS PUGH: (*Voice off.*) You put that on and you're in trouble!

HUW: Can I go out then?

MRS PUGH: (*Voice off.*) You've just been out!

HUW: But I went to get the wireless!

MRS PUGH: (*Voice off.*) Shut up about that wireless! I've had enough of it!

HUW: Well what am I supposed to do?

MRS PUGH: (*Voice off.*) Be a man!

HUW: I'll go out.

MRS PUGH: (*Voice off.*) You go outside that door and you can sleep in the street!

(*Silence.*)

HUW: I know. I'll take the wireless back.

MRS PUGH: (*Voice off.*) Whose is it?

HUW: Twm's.

MRS PUGH: (*Voice off.*) Well didn't Twm want to listen to it?

HUW: Yes. He's listening on Dai's.

MRS PUGH: (*Voice off.*) You're not going round that Dai's! His wife's a tart.

HUW: I wouldn't dream of it..

MRS PUGH: (*Voice off.*) You'd better mind you don't or I'll stop you sleeping! Right! You've got four minutes!

HUW: Four minutes? Why four minutes?

MRS PUGH: (*Voice off.*) Because I said so!

(*HUW looks bemused. He picks up the wireless and leaves. We hear MRS PUGH snoring again.*)

Scene 2

Later

HUW comes on drunk. He is having some difficulty standing. He puts a finger to his lips and says: 'Sssshhh!' Silence. We can hear MRS PUGH snoring.

HUW: (*To the audience.*) That's buggered it! Dylan has gone and put me in his play! Plotting to poison my wife. In the play! For everybody to hear! When she finds out she'll gut me. If I'm here. So I'll have to go. I suppose. (*Pause.*) Went round to Dai's. Few flagons we had. His wife's a lovely tart. She brings out a bottle of whiskey. I could see her garters. Bending over she was. For the bottle. The boys were in a state of high tumour. (*Pause. Thinks. Fearfully.*) He's cursed me! That's what he has done! Twm said it, Dai said it, Dai's lovely tarty wife said it – they all said it together: 'Huw! That damn Dylan has cursed you boy just as soon as if it was a witch's spit. Because he's the only one who could tell you why he wrote it and he's dead! And people will always give the benefit of the doubt to the dead!' (*Pause.*)

Why did he do it? I know a lot of the time we all hated
the sod but there's no need to be so bloody nasty!
Now I'll have to go. But I don't know where to go or
even which way to go. If I go West or South that's the
sea and I haven't got a boat and if I go North it's the
mountains and I'm not a goat, so I must go East. There's
nowhere else TO go! (*Pause.*) I'll go back to Swansea.
I am a Swansea boy! God, this is ruination!
(*HUW goes to the bottom of the stairs and looks up.*)
Listen!
(*Sound of MRS PUGH snoring.*)
That's not the sound of a great wife. That's the sound of
a great white!
(*While looking upstairs, he points a finger and shakes it.*)
Yes! You're right Mrs Pugh! I am indistinctive AND
stinking. Who can blame me when I've been blown
around the house by the tail end of my wife's gales?
Now I'll just have to see where the wind blows me!
(*HUW finds his bag already packed – he looks into it
quickly.*)
A-ha! That old game is it? Think I'll come crawling up
the stairs to you! For forgiveness! Begging to stay!
Submit myself to the vice of your jaws! Not this time!
Dylan's made sure of that!
(*He picks up his bag and leaves.*
Lights down.
In the dark, MRS PUGH cries out.
As she speaks, the lights come up and we see HUW.)

MRS PUGH: (*Voice off.*) He's gone! To look for some
athletic girl I suppose! Some tart who'll show her knickers
for a penny to any pleading dirty man. Or maybe he
listened to that play of Dylan's on the radio and became
envious of his fame so that the little world of his life and
wife couldn't hold him. But where will you go little Huw
Pugh? To the big towns of the East? Swansea? Cardiff?
Newport? No! You'll get no further than the pub which is
where I'll find you, mark my words!

Scene 3a

Next morning. Railway station

HUW is laying down like a bundle in his mac.

HUW: That night I slept on the station. Just as the train gets in, head infested with a nation of red ants, Gladys, the wife's friend, turns up on her way to Carmarthen. (*GLADYS comes on and kicks HUW in the back.*) Ow!

GLADYS: Huw Pugh you disgusting boil! I heard something on the radio last night that I'm too ashamed to talk about!

HUW: Shurrup then! And don't you kick me or I'll throw you under the train!

GLADYS: I heard that you want to kill your wife! To poison her like a common rat! Taking your wife arsenic – for breakfast! And that was after killing the poor parakeet!

HUW: We never had a parakeet! He's lying! He made it all up!

GLADYS: Huh! It's easy to say that now he's dead! He's not here to defend himself!

HUW: No! And he's not here for me to challenge him either!

GLADYS: You poisoning snake! Look at you quivering and wet in the flood of your own underpants! You've peed yourself!

HUW: That's because you kicked me in the kidneys!

GLADYS: You deserve it! And what about the book: 'Lives of the Great Poisoners!'

HUW: Lie!

GLADYS: And what about the gruel of unbelievable poisons unknown to man or rat that would cement her inside so that she would die because of the building growing in her? It must be true because it's so poetic!!

HUW: No! It's the lying that makes it poetic!

GLADYS: If I was you I'd take this train to the end of the line and never come back because once I get home she'll hear all about it from me!

(*She kicks HUW again and leaves.*
HUW cries out.
Sound of train.
We hear the voice of MRS PUGH.)

MRS PUGH: (*Voice off. Bitterly.*) I traipsed every last street and back alley of our little town, every jut and jetty, every pier, every last groin, every and any protuberance of land or promontory into the sea on that sad simple Sunday, for it was on Sunday Pugh left knocking the stuffing out of all our future chicken dinners, to find him, my feckless bleak spouse. And on that Monday, school was shut and I was thrown out of home like sick from the mouth onto the street.

Scene 3b

Spring 1954. Mumbles

HUW is a tram conductor: blazer. He stands on the stairs as though on the platform of a tram.

HUW: So I took the train to Swansea.
(*He puts on a conductor's cap.*)
But when I got here I didn't know what to do! Then I saw a poster. Hold tight please! Next stop Mumbles pier! Plenty of room inside! Full upstairs! (*To the audience.*) The poster said: 'Don't know what to do? Be a conductor on the Mumbles tram'! I thought: why not? Only, I can't climb the stairs because of the curse laid on me by the play which had the fictitious me climb the morning stairs with my murderous fancy! And so I can't collect fares on the upper deck! Plenty of room inside! Full upstairs!
(*A LITTLE OLD LADY with hand bag comes on and stands before HUW.*)

LITTLE OLD LADY: What you on about, mun? There's more room up there than in the Gobi desert! Unless they're all lying flat on the upper deck!

HUW: I'm expecting a mumble of nuns who've asked for the top deck to be nearer to God.

LITTLE OLD LADY: Nuns on the Mumbles mun? Never! Not on the tram!

HUW: Alright, then. Party of school children. Small heads on low bodies.

LITTLE OLD LADY: You're a lying lout! You just don't want to climb! I'm going to report you to the Corporation!

HUW: You have no sense of the fantastic!

LITTLE OLD LADY: O yes I have! I loved Dylan Thomas's play! I heard it two nights ago and it made me so excited I've had the runs ever since! It's a masterpiece!

HUW: Not much to show for a thousand bardic years! Dwelling on the small miseries of school teachers and the peccadilloes of sightless sea captains! I don't want you on my tram you simple Welsh sycophant!

LITTLE OLD LADY: Let me on!

HUW: No! You reeking boil and bed-soiled doting Dylan crone! (*To the audience in shock.*) You see?! The play has got me! I've become a poet!

LITTLE OLD LADY: Lemme on!

(*She pulls at HUW.*)

HUW: Gerroff!

LITTLE OLD LADY: Lemme up the stairs!

HUW: Gerroff!

(*LITTLE OLD LADY pulls HUW off the tram and swings her handbag at him. He catches the bag and pulls her towards him.*)

I don't want to do this!

(*She comes towards him and he – accidentally – head-butts her. She lets out a terrible scream and falls to floor. HUW is jumping around in despair and confusion.*)

LITTLE OLD LADY: (*Holding her head. Tearful.*)

You shouldn't've done that! Especially if you didn't want to do it! I've got twelve angry sons who will get you! If I was you I'd get out of Swansea. Go as far as you can! Go to America I would!

(*HUW stands frozen for a moment.
Lights down except for a light on HUW.*)

HUW: (*Tearfully.*) America! I'll have to. Now that this has
    happened! I'll go to New York. Where Dylan died.
    Why not? Things can't get worse!
    (*Lights down.*)
    And so I embarked at Southampton for the New World.

Scene 4

Summer 1954. On board ship

*Sound of ship's hooter etc. HUW is at the front of the ship looking
out at the Atlantic.*

HUW: We steamed out in the Summer of '54 for New York,
    sun blazing and a light, brackish offshore breeze.
    (*Sound of the sea.*)
    I felt full of myself and full, too, of that insolent little
    claret they gave us with lunch! We navigated the English
    Channel, departing Britannia at my right hand, my brow
    bejewelled with the deliquescence of a rising passion.
    By night fall...
    (*Lights down a little.*)
    ...still proud at prow, face fast against the Atlantic
    spray and behind me the lights and tintinnabulation of
    the seabound revellers, deciding to evacuate the dark
    which threatened to displace my wine-boldness,
    I turned and...
    (*SINEAD comes and stands behind HUW.*)
SINEAD: (*Irish accent.*) Can you tell me the way to
    New York?
    (*HUW lets out a cry and falls back onto the rail; SINEAD
    pulls him to stop him falling overboard.*)
    Sure I didn't mean to frighten you like that!
HUW: (*Angrily.*) You sneaked up on me in the dark!
SINEAD: I was trying to be friendly!
HUW: What are you? Irish?!
SINEAD: I am that!
HUW: Only the Irish would ask the way to New York on a
    boat that's going there!

SINEAD: It was supposed to be a joke! And you should
be careful what you say about people's nationality.
WELSHman! I've heard that the Welsh can be
quite shifty.

HUW: Shifty?!

SINEAD: For generations you have entertained the English!
Making laugh the people you hate!
(*Pause.*)

HUW: Well as it happens, I hate the Welsh!

SINEAD: O, and why is that?

HUW: Because, my little Miss cockles and mussels, they
have put a curse on me. Well…not the whole nation: one
in particular.

SINEAD: In what way have they cursed you?

HUW: You wouldn't understand.

SINEAD: O, I might, for I am in my own way cursed.

HUW: You're just saying that.

SINEAD: I am not! I am from the North of Ireland but I'm
a Catholic. THAT is to be cursed!

HUW: Pffffffft!

SINEAD: Okay, so what's yours?

HUW: The curse of a dead man!

SINEAD: It doesn't make sense.

HUW: I've been written into a book. I'll be in there forever!
I can never be written out!

SINEAD: You should be flattered.

HUW: Flattered? I'm flattened! I could have been a hero,
instead I'm a snake!

SINEAD: You've been written of in a book as a snake?

HUW: Not an actual snake, no! A man who ACTS like
a snake.

SINEAD: I must admit that does seem a little mischievous.

HUW: Ineluctable, mun!

SINEAD: Have you got the book with you?
(*HUW takes out the book and gives it to her.*)
Under Milk Wood. (*She looks inside.*) A play for voices.
(*She throws book overboard.*
HUW is shocked to silence.)

75

There you are! Now it's UNDER THE SEA! You should never let yourself be cursed by a play!
(*HUW lets out a terrible cry.*
He begins pulling at his clothes and hair, making a terrible noise. He falls to his knees.)
Stop it! Please! Stop! This is crazy!
(*She gets on her knees beside HUW and takes him at the shoulders and shakes him gently. He is crying.*)

HUW: Now I'll be cursed for ever and never get away from it!

SINEAD: No! I'm sorry, I'm sorry! It was only a book. I didn't know it would have this effect. If I could throw my country into the sea to get rid of the curse it puts on not just me but so many, I would! I'd throw the whole thing in!
(*Pause.*)
Never mind a book.
(*Silence.*
HUW calms a little.)
What was it even about?

HUW: (*Sniffing.*) It's not about anything. Not anything in particular. Just a village waking up and going back to sleep.

SINEAD: Well, that's it then! It's a curse because it's got you all lathered up about nothing. It's a strange people who can be held in the grip of a play about nothing when the likes of us are cursed by a real and terrible history. O that we were cursed by plays in Ireland.

HUW: (*Miserable.*) Except, you can run away from a country. For ever.

SINEAD: I'm not running away; I'm no coward. I'm exercising my discretion.

HUW: I wish I COULD be a coward and successfully escape all the miseries of my life.

SINEAD: O you poor little man! You're like a child! I'm being too harsh on you. Don't worry! We're cursed together! You from your country, me from mine.
(*She holds him tentatively.*)

My country is crippled by its past. I want to live in the
future! That's why I'm going to New York. I'm throwing
all my past overboard.
(*Silence.*)

HUW: There was a young woman from Limerick
Who thought she was going to be seasick
So she went to the prow
Where she is now
And made a Welshman's heart quick.

SINEAD: That's sweet. Did you make that up this minute?

HUW: Yes.

SINEAD: Except I'm not from Limerick.

HUW: No, but the limerick is!

SINEAD: What's your name?

HUW: Huw. (*Short pause.*) Pugh.

SINEAD: Huw or Pugh?

HUW: Both. Huw and Pugh. Huw Pugh.

SINEAD: Okay, Huw Pugh...

HUW: No. Just Huw if you...

SINEAD: Huw...

HUW: Pugh is my surname. My name, my Christian name
is Huw...

SINEAD: Huw...
(*HUW moves towards SINEAD and tries to kiss her. She resists.*)
Hey not so fast! I've heard about you Welshmen!
Baby-makers!

HUW: I only want a kiss mun!

SINEAD: S-s-s-s-hhhhh!

HUW: Just a peck!

SINEAD: Quiet!

HUW: Why? What?

SINEAD: That noise.
(*HUW looks up.*)

HUW: There's a bit of a wind got up.

SINEAD: It's more than that!
(*Silence.*
*Suddenly the sound of a huge storm. They sit staring mouths
agape ahead of them. There is lightning etc. and they are in
the thick of a huge storm.*

Inside the sound of the storm we hear The Voices.
They hold onto each other tightly.)

HUW: (*Shouting above storm.*) I'm scared! Let's go inside!

SINEAD: (*Also shouting.*) We can't move! If we do we'll get thrown over! Just sit tight!

HUW: O Mam! Mam!

SINEAD: Mam?!

HUW: I should never have left the small lapping waves of home! These waves are like mountains!
(*There should be lights flashing, sound of high wind, The Voices etc.*
SINEAD and HUW should be moving as if on a stormy sea.)

SINEAD: (*Still shouting.*) They can get up to eighty foot high! My Da was in the Navy in the war and he said they hit some in mid-ocean that were so big the ship had to CLIMB them before going on down the other side!

HUW: I don't think I want to hear this now! We will end up drowned and our sinews twisted like sea-wrack, lives wrecked by the curse of Milk Wood! And it's all your fault!

SINEAD: It's just a storm! It's got nothing to do with any curse!

HUW: (*Looking ahead of him with mad, staring eyes and pointing.*) What's that?!

SINEAD: That my salty sea dog is a WALL OF WATER! GET DOWN!!!!!!!!!!!
(*Sound of crashing waves.*
The Voices become a hollow loud howl.
Lights snap off.)

Scene 5

New York Port

(*Music from 'West Side Story' suddenly erupting.*)

Lots of noise; ships' hooters, people cheering, train whistles etc.

SINEAD comes on looking bedraggled.

HUW follows her on, head bowed, almost dragging his bag. He looks lonely and lost.

SINEAD stops and looks around her. She speaks with a slight American accent.

HUW: Where will you go?

SINEAD: I told you! I've got a relation who's going to give me a job in his bar.

(*As they speak they don't look at each other.*)

HUW: You didn't tell me.

SINEAD: (*With irony.*) Well forgive me! If you recall… what's the point?…

HUW: You haven't spoken to me for a week.

SINEAD: The last time there were words between us you blamed me for that wave!

HUW: It's just that it was a new experience for me! I grew up paddling in Pendine!

SINEAD: Well if you confront every new experience in such a catastrophic way, you'd better get the next boat back because AMERICA will be a crisis a minute for you! Taxi!

HUW: Can I come with you?

SINEAD: Don't be crazy! You'd be a burden on my back like that play is on yours! You can't face change.
You enjoy that curse because it gives you a link with your past. Taxi!

HUW: It's called hiraeth!

SINEAD: Call it what you like. It's like never washing your underwear.

HUW: I'll give it up! Right now!

SINEAD: Forget it!

HUW: (*Pleadingly.*) Sinead!

SINEAD: Listen! You hear my accent? It's American already. I practised. On the ship. There's too much at stake for me. I ain't gonna let my future get diseased by my past.
Where I come from the highlight of the year for most people is to march to celebrate some battle they fought hundreds of years before. That's Northern Ireland for you. It's choking on its past! I'm headin' out for tomorrow!

79

HUW: What will I do?
(*She goes to him.*
She puts a hand to his face.)
SINEAD: (*Softly.*) You'll make it kid. Don't worry.
HUW: Where will I go?
SINEAD: Well, if you got nowhere else, try the YMCA.
I gotta get this cab. So long kid.
(*She leaves.*
HUW sits despondently.)

Scene 6

Central Park, New York

HUW is laying down in sleeping bag. He has a book open face down on his chest.

HUW: (*To the audience.*) I, in the centre of Central Park
could lie and await the crows to eat me. Me, leaner now
for passing time – Listen! That's time passing! – leaner
in body and mind: leaner like deciduous winter boughs.
Ants are deciduous, shedding their wings after
copulation. I exist in a state of having shed. I am the
constant shedder. I am lonely, hungry with hiraeth;
hungry for hills. In this mood, I, yesterday, went into a
book shop on Fifty-third Street. I have had two weeks of
sleeping rough in the unWelsh womb of New York after
my beautiful colleen cleaned out my heart and
NEEDED, NEEDED to put myself in the company of
Welshness. So: I bought a copy of the play.
(*He holds up book.*)
I've been reading it all night. Why was Dylan so spiteful
to me? Was I so insolent? Did I let drop in his company
some hint of discontent? I read and I can't see clearly!
I am torn between hiraeth and hatred! How I hate the
low moaning meanness of hills! ALSO: I bought this
book about him.
(*HUW holds up a different book.*)
About Dylan. It names the pub in which he drank the
eighteen whiskies that, it's said, killed him. LINED up

on the bar. I will go there and with the little I have left
of money and humanity, finally alone and lonely, I will
line up NINETEEN whiskies and drink them and
though, maybe, dead, will be over Dylan, over Wales,
over ME and OVER MILK WOOD! So:

Scene 7

New York Bar

*Behind the bar is SINEAD. She speaks with an American accent.
She's eating peanuts: flicking them up and catching them in her
mouth. At the bar is JACK. He is hunched up over a drink.*

SINEAD: (*To JACK.*) Sure I felt sorry for the little Welsh guy.

JACK: Hey, Sinead! I know you and you don't feel sorry
for no one, okay? He, he!

SINEAD: Okay, but I could empathise. I could tell he
didn't feel he belonged anywhere.

JACK: Whad is this belongs? Who belongs? I don't wanna
belong! Next thing, you've reindruduced slavery!

SINEAD: Okay! So maybe that's it. Maybe he THINKS he
should belong and because he don't he feels he's missing
something whereas he should just not want to belong
anyway.

JACK: Don't belong! Thass my motto!

SINEAD: Yeh, well okay Jack but it's a bit different because
who would want you to belong TO them?

JACK: Yeh! You god a point there, Sinead. He, he, he.

SINEAD: When I was Irish, I was a Catholic in the North
and I didn't feel like I belonged because I wanted to
belong to the South and the North ain't in the South.

JACK: Thass my point! Double bourbon Bud chaser.

SINEAD: Yeh, okay. In a minute. I juss wish I'd been a bit
nicer to the little guy, thass all.

JACK: If you'da been nicer maybe he'da ended up belonging
to you and all that stuff.

SINEAD: Yeh, well... I mean, he blamed me for that wave
on the boat 'cos I threw his book away. But thass just

looking for excuses in a crisis. I think the real reason
was I wouldn't let him kiss me.

JACK: See? The guy's a fiend! Gimme a beef salad over rye.

SINEAD: (*Shouts to off.*) Beef salad over rye! (*To JACK.*)
Anyway, I miss him. I do. Funny little guy. Okay. You
could say this guy had no brains or no wisdom. Like...
no digging of life's bum deals but what he had was soul
and soul you cannot buy not for a million bucks.

JACK: Look: What's brought all this on is that I pointed
out to you dat plaque over there which was put up in
memory of dat guy who drunk all those whiskies in this
bar that killed him – that same guy who...

SINEAD: ...wrote the book. Yeh, I know. Dylan. And I was
shocked because I never noticed it because The Man
Mountain was always sitting in that chair! Yeh, the guy
just came in here, lined eighteen whiskies up on the bar
and just knocked them back...
(*HUW shuffles on.*)
Jees!

JACK: Whad is it? Whad?

SINEAD: Iss him! Huw!

JACK: Whad? Dis bum?

SINEAD: Shurrup, Jack!
(*When HUW sees her he stops and they both just look at each
other in silence for a moment.*)

HUW: Nineteen whiskies please.
(*She faces him, shocked.*)

SINEAD: You!

HUW: You!
(*Silence.*)
Nineteen whiskies please.

SINEAD: I know what this is, kid.

HUW: Nineteen whiskies please.

SINEAD: This is where it happened. See that plaque?
(*HUW turns and looks out at audience.*
He turns back to her.)

HUW: Nineteen whiskies, please.

SINEAD: You know what happened to him!

HUW: Nineteen whiskies please.

SINEAD: No!

HUW: I know what I'm doing. I've GOT to do this!
This one thing. Definite. I've got to find out who I am.

SINEAD: You drink nineteen whiskies and you won't even
remember that you ever were!

HUW: Come on Sinead!

(*Pause.*)

SINEAD: Okay. Let's do it!

(*She puts another glass on the bar.*)

(*To JACK.*) Hey, you know who this guy is?

JACK: Yeh! You juss said. The Welsh guy who's in the book.

SINEAD: Yeh. That book written by the other Welsh guy...

JACK: Yeh, yeh! Dylan. The one what we was just talking
about. Happened two years ago. So what?

SINEAD: Well THAT guy drank eighteen whiskies, THIS
guy wants to drink nineteen.

JACK: Yeh? Thad'll be the day.

SINEAD: You don't think he can do it?

JACK: O yeh. I think he could do it if you god him to the
floor and poured the stuff down his throat! But on his
own? I'd pud some serious bucks on that he can't!

SINEAD: What? You want me to open a book?

JACK: Sure!

SINEAD: I'll give you fifty to one says he can do it!

JACK: You're on.

(*HUW is staring at SINEAD. He begins to shake, his teeth
chattering.*
Pause.)

SINEAD: (*Staring at HUW.*) Forget it. He ain't gonna do it.
You don't need this Huw.

HUW: O, Sinead! What are you doing here?

SINEAD: This is the place I told you about!

HUW: It's unbe... Could I have ONE whisky?

SINEAD: Sure.

(*She leaves a glass on bar and fills it.*
HUW gulps it down.)

HUW: Could I have another one?

SINEAD: (*Laughing.*) Hey, don't think you're gonna get the
nineteen this way!

(*She fills his glass.*)

Anyway, I thought you were going to leave that whole play and curse thing behind!

HUW: I was homesick.

(*He gulps the drink.*)

SINEAD: Take it easy!

HUW: One more?

SINEAD: Last one.

(*She pours the drink.*)

You know? I missed you.

(*He gulps it down.*

HUW is beginning to sway a little and his speech is uncertain.)

HUW: Sinead. This is fate.

SINEAD: Sure is coincidental!

(*Pause.*)

HUW: Sinead. I would love to be your...hubsand.

SINEAD: My hubsand huh?

HUW: Did I say that? (*He giggles.*)

SINEAD: You slid on it!

JACK: Hey Joe, I couldn't help overhearing you.

SINEAD: His name is Huw.

JACK: Okay, so his name's Huw! Wass the difference to a no-hoper who's asking for your hand in holy matribolony?

HUW: Wass it got to do with you?

SINEAD: Leave it Huw. Jack, just shurrup! (*Cheerfully.*)

Anyway, how do I know you're not already married?

HUW: Mumummarriedme?

SINEAD: Yeh.

HUW: I...um...no... No... I'm...n...

SINEAD: Hey, wait a minute. I think you are!

(*HUW pauses. He pulls himself together a little unsteadily.*

He begins to speak with authority – sounding like Dylan.)

JACK: The guy's a bigamist! Iss all over his face!

HUW: I was.

JACK: What? You was a bigamist or you was married?!

HUW: (*Angrily.*) She died.

SINEAD: Died? Hey, I'm sorry...

JACK: Yeh, okay. I didn' know. How'd she go?

HUW: She was poisoned. A drink? Please?
(*SINEAD pours him a drink.*
He takes a sip.)
It happened… One night she had to go into the cellar –
into the dark doom-worried depths of the cellar where
she kept the tools of her preoccupation which was
gardening, to get the rake to rake the garden which she
had weeded in the afternoon of that day, that deathly day.
There was a light switch at the top of the stairs, stairs
which flew like a bat swooping into the blackness of its
habitat which she switched on and began to make her
descent. Suddenly, out of nowhere the sky filled with
great billows of dark haunted clouds like a coal miner's
coal dyed pillows and a storm betokening more calamity
than the storm that broke over the head of the dying
Christ, broke over our house! Lightning struck and all
the lights were killed just as my marvellous wife was in
mid step. She slipped, went down the stairs like a boy
on a toboggan, and came to rest in a plate full of rat
poison that I had put down only that morning. She was
unconscious but breathing and unhappily imbibed the
deadly dust until she died and I thought all through this
time of her dying that she was in the garden raking up
the effects of her endeavours.
JACK: Jees! What a way to go!
(*SINEAD takes HUW's hands.*)
SINEAD: That's so sad!
HUW: Shelter me from life's storms! I will love YOU till the
rivers run dry and the wind around the Black Mountain
becomes a murmur at the far end of the universe.
AND I will love you, Sinead, until the cows come home.
SINEAD: It would be like marrying a choir full of
landscapes!
(*HUW collapses.*)
Huw!
JACK: Looks like you god anudder dead un!
(*Lights down.*
In the dark, the sound of wedding bells.)

Scene 8a

Outside New York apartment

SINEAD is sitting on top of a fire-escape stairs. It's a hot summer evening. Sounds of the city. She is speaking with an exaggerated New York accent.

SINEAD: (*To the audience.*) He was okay. He sobered up and we got married! I tell you one thing about these Welsh guys: they sure know how to make babies. I'm pregnant and O God, I just think it's great! You'll've figured we got married. (*She breathes deep.*) And I love it here! De Bronx! Smell dose smells! I'm still woikin at the bar while Huw, he got this job in a shop which sells stuff about Wales. Yeh. Wales is big ever since the writer popped it. Dat gets me! Dis guy was a real clown! Used to come over here to read poems to really big audiences. Sounded like some opera star or somethin'. Anyway, they'd throw dinner parties before the show and he'd get smashed and HE'd throw da hostess over his shoulder! And they'd all be like so embarrassed and he'd be like this puffy balloon type guy. So, anyway, he does the deed in that bar I woik in – drunk the eighteen whiskies – two days later he's dead in St Vincent's Hospital and suddenly his COUNTRY is on the map! Dis is the country Huw makes dis big thing of! So: what I want to know is – what kind of country is that?
(*TONY comes on as if being pursued by someone.*)
Hey Tony!
(*TONY stops, looking about him warily.*)
What kind of country is that where it's unknown but then its poet dies in his puke and it becomes woild famous? What kind of country is dat?
TONY: I dunno! Maybe's somewhere over in New Joisey!
SINEAD: (*To the audience.*) He don't know! Ha! (*To TONY.*) Hey Tony! New Joisey is like New York! Iss juss a town! Schmuck! He, he, he!

TONY: So whaddo I know? Why you aksin' me? I majored in auto theft not geometery or whatever it is where you know about places! I done even know where Idaly is! I'm a Bronx boy! Why done you aks your ole man? Ain't he from over there someplace?

SINEAD: Hey! If I coulda asked him I wouldna had the question!

TONY: Jees! You guys! Hey, I know whad I was gonna say. Whad is it wid your ole man dat e's got to do all this screamin' at night? You know: this wakes up mi amore!

SINEAD: Yeh, I know. Iss dat guy again.

TONY: Whad guy? Somebody botherin' you two? You want I take his legs off?

SINEAD: He's dead.

TONY: Okay. So where's he buried?

SINEAD: No, no. Iss okay. Iss somethin you wouldn' get, Tony. This guy who is now dead, wrote a play that he put Huw in. Iss jess memories, thass all. It's jess like – it puts this cloud hanging over everything and it makes Huw, you know, kind of introvoit so I don't know what he's thinking. It makes it difficult to tell him about the baby.

TONY: Whad baby?

SINEAD: I'm gonna have a baby!

TONY: Hey, dass great! You wait till I tell Anna!

SINEAD: Well don't tell Anna till I tole Huw!

TONY: Hey! I'm not gonna tell nobody nuthin'!

SINEAD: Here he comes now! Home from woik!

(*HUW comes to the bottom of stairs carrying a box.*)

Hi Huw!

HUW: (*Pleasantly.*) Hi Sinead.

SINEAD: You look beat hun.

HUW: It's okay. I'm not used to the metropolitan summer. The heat sticks to you like burnt sugar.

TONY: So. I gotta love you and leave you kids. But just let me say, Huw...whad is it?... Congratulations!

(*HUW looks bemused.*)

SINEAD: I was...um...just telling Tony about our wedding.

TONY: Yeh! Sure! Ha, ha!

(*TONY leaves. HUW sits at the bottom of stairs.*)

SINEAD: Remember? You said we had no confetti or rice but we had angel dust which settled on you like snow and I picked up handfuls of it and threw it in your face! (*They both laugh.*)

HUW: And your laughter was so full-faced your teeth were like a row of whitewashed adobes on a far-off mountain in Mexico...

SINEAD: ...and I thought: this is it! We're married! We will inherit sunbeams baby! I was like Cleopatra. And then we got this apartment.

HUW: Aye! Next to a fire escape! It's so small it makes the fire escape look like the main feature!

SINEAD: (*Still playfully.*) Look at him! The moaner! I think it was a mistake I married you! We had a fling – a romantic fling on board ship. That was it!

HUW: (*Also light-heartedly.*) We were almost flung into the sea! That's all! What fling?

SINEAD: Well okay! A moment! But sometimes when you're, like, all at sea in time, a moment can seem like something to hang onto! Anyway, it seemed to me, little honey, that you had suffered. And then in the bar and you told me the story about your wife and how...
(*HUW suddenly jumps up.*)

HUW: Don't talk about that Sinead! Please?

SINEAD: Okay hun.
(*HUW moves up a step.*
Pause.)

HUW: (*Sadly.*) Did you have any mountains in Northern Ireland?

SINEAD: Why?

HUW: Just wondering.

SINEAD: Well...they got the mountains of Mourne.

HUW: You see! I knew it! It's so sad. So sorrowful. So...so poetic. In Wales we've got Plynlimmon, The Presselis, the dark Black Mountains, the barren and bleak Beacons, Cader Idris and Mighty Snowdon!

SINEAD: Forget it! Forget all that! You know what we got over here? We got The Appalachians! The Alleghenies!

The Sierra Nevadas! We got The Blue Mountains,
The Big Horn Mountains, The Sacramento Mountains,
The Shoshone Mountains and The Bitteroot Mountains!
And then a-course, we got The Rocky Mountains and
The Black Hills of Dakota! Sometimes, Huw, you make
me angry! Thinking about those mountains of Wales.
You should sit out here some nights and listen to the
downtown city! The rhythms of this city would shock
you instead of this munching on the moon! You should
find out about America! LEARN about America 'cos
that's where we are now! What's in the box?
(*HUW begins to climb stairs.*)

HUW: A dragon.

SINEAD: A dragon? Let me see.
(*HUW takes out a big toy dragon.*
He gives it to SINEAD.)

SINEAD: What IS this?

HUW: It's a Welsh dragon. For you.

SINEAD: That's really nice hun, but...

HUW: (*Suddenly oratorical.*) This dragon will save my soul!
The dragon burns the night with its breath of fire and
breaks through to the myths of days and fabulous echoes:
choruses of the insubstantial of Eastern philosophies of
gods and more and heralds robed in undreamable weave.
I would, if I had the power of fable replace the Manhattan
Indians in Manhattan and retire the Hudson to run for
eternity as an unnameable waterway; I would unrealise the
real and patch from the tatters of dreams a tapestry of
imagined phenomena.
(*HUW goes off.*)

SINEAD: This I don't like. This is beginning to look like a
mountain of blues. (*To HUW off.*) We need more of the
stuff about the Manhattan Indians, Huw. And've you
been practising de woids like I said? You know you
USED to say tomato now you say toMAto?

HUW: (*With Welsh accent, off.*) But I always say tomato!

SINEAD: And you don't say 'I think', you say 'I guess'.

HUW: (*Off.*) I suppose so.

SINEAD: No! Not suppose neither! 'Guess!' I say: you don't say 'I think' you say 'I guess' and you say 'I guess so' if you don't want to say straight 'yes'. And if you see a beggar on the street, he ain't no beggar he's a BUM. Say it.

HUW: (*Off.*) Bum.

SINEAD: Yeh, but say it, you know, like it's something dropping heavily to the floor. BUM!

HUW: (*Off.*) Bum!

SINEAD: And anudder thing: some day, here in the heart of the Bronx or maybe, who knows we may even move out West – someday we gonna want some kids wouldn't you guess?

HUW: (*Off.*) Yes

SINEAD: And dese kids is gonna want to loin some and in the meantime YOU need to loin some about dis country we're now in so that when the kids come you're ready for 'em. You guess?

HUW: (*Off.*) Yes.

SINEAD: Okay. So I think one thing – we should start a library. And I got notified of a special offer today of dis book club which you can collect dis encyclopaedia of American history and when you get the first volume you get free dis book called 'Lives Of The Great Poisoners'.
(*HUW lets out a terrible cry off.*
SINEAD gets up.)
Huw! What is it? (*To the audience.*) O Jees, I got it: what a schmuck I am. Poisoners! His wife…
(*HUW comes to top of stairs.*
He is shaking.
TONY comes to the bottom of the staircase.)
(*Now with her Irish accent.*) Huw! What is it? You're shaking!

TONY: Whad is it? Wass all the noise? Sounds like someone's havin' his throat slit!

SINEAD: It's okay Tony.

HUW: Too much to bear! Too much to bear!

SINEAD: What is? What is it?

HUW: All the dead, dear drowned of Nantucket...

TONY: De guy's gone bananas!

SINEAD: Tony! Shut it!

(*SINEAD takes hold of him and helps him sit.*)

Huw, you're frightening me! This isn't making sense!

(*HUW sits and she sits with him and holds him.*)

HUW: I don't know. Perhaps it's the wave. Haunting me.
It's like: you're afraid of going to sleep in case you stop
breathing. My head is full of – WORDS! Words which
just want to come out even though you don't want them
to! (*Howls.*) Utah!

SINEAD: Utah? Utah's a state! An American state!

HUW: Utah Watkins! Drowned in his drawers smelling of
parsley! See? I don't want to say it! What parsley?

TONY: You wanna know what parsley? The parsley dat's
growing out through your ears from the brain in your
head! If you don't shurrup my kids are gonna grow up
mentally defoimed!

SINEAD: Leave it, Tone!

TONY: Okay but you juss quieten him down!

(*TONY goes.*)

HUW: The white bone talking! Nantucket's graveyard!
The quaker dead! (*Singing.*) Knickers in a jar on a
Sunday morning, O what a beautiful sight to see!

SINEAD: Stop it! This is because of the play! It must be.
Huw tell me! Have you been reading it?

(*HUW looks at her like a lost boy.*)

HUW: No Mam. I haven't been reading IT. It reads me!
It takes me over!

SINEAD: Where is it?

HUW: I haven't got it Mam! Honest!

(*Pause.*)

Too much to bear! Ebeneezer's bell! Ebeneezer's bell
tolls for the tiddlers and drowned tiddler fish of men!
We die of blisters! We die of blisters!

(*SINEAD gets up.*)

SINEAD: HUW! Shurrup! I've got something to tell you.

HUW: I'll try and get some sleep.

SINEAD: (*Suddenly hopeful.*) Yes! (*Pause.*) Are you alright?

HUW: Sure I am hun.

SINEAD: You spoke some American!

HUW: I've just got an over-active mind.

SINEAD: I think that's right!

HUW: Dylan wasn't blind but he still saw inside the slutty moonless night.

SINEAD: Are you sure you haven't got the book?

HUW: No! It's all in there. (*Points to his head.*) It's a cold, corpse night in the black mind: the bleak, cracked raven black mind!

SINEAD: Let me take you to bed, Huw. (*To the audience.*) I can't tell him yet. It'll have to be later.
(*They go off.*
Lights down.)

Scene 8b

Later. Night. Low lights

HUW is at top of the stairs, reading.

SINEAD comes on though he doesn't see her.

SINEAD: So I went to work and when I came home, there he was sitting at the top of the fire escape reading. I got as close as I could without him seeing me to see what it was that he was reading for I was afraid! And that fear bore a bitter fruit. And there he was looking out to the East – looking out across the Atlantic to Wales, I guess! – reading:

HUW: ...'By Carreg Cennen, King of time,
Our Heron Head is only
A bit of stone with seaweed spread
Where gulls come to be lonely.
A tiny dingle is Milk Wood
By Golden Grove 'neath Grongar,
But let me choose and oh! I should
Love all my life the longer...'

(*Looking up from bottom of stairs.*) Huw! You promised!

HUW: What are you doing spying on me?

SINEAD: I wasn't spying, I just happened…

HUW: (*Suddenly shouting he begins coming down stairs.*)
You're like some worm! A rag worm or lug worm,
some enormous conger eel of a worm worming its way
in the gaps in my mind, worming around in my
thoughts, a moby haunting worm like the worm that
eats up the eyes of the sailors who drowned bringing
YOU treasures…

TONY: (*Off.*) Hey, shurrup over there!

SINEAD: The book!

HUW: It's fine! The book is fine! The book… YOU you
were sent…

SINEAD: Stop it! You're frightening me!

HUW: You were sent to wash away in seas the comfort of
my views!

TONY: (*Off.*) You want me to call the cops?

SINEAD: I don't know what that means!
(*Silence.*
*He is above her now. He looks mad. Suddenly he raises his
arm high and brings the book crashing down on her head.*)

HUW: It means you're ruining my life!
(*We see TONY standing near bottom of staircase.*
Lights down immediately. SINEAD lets out a cry.
In the darkness we hear an echoing scream.
We also hear The Voices and the sound of feet running.
There is a blue light flashing.)
(*In the dark.*) You can't arrest me! I didn't try to kill
my wife! Why would I want to kill my wife?!
You can't kill someone with a play! What kind of
world are we living in? This is madness! Gerroff me,
I'm a free man!

TONY: (*Off.*) Throw away the key!

Scene 9

Hospital

HUW is sitting slumped forward in a chair.

Silence.

SINEAD comes on. HUW turns away from her.

SINEAD: Huw. I don't understand any of this. They've got you in here for trying to kill me! But only because Tony told them that that's what it looked like to him. But this is crazy! Tell me you didn't really want to hurt me!
(*Silence.*

SINEAD falls to her knees beside HUW and holds his hands.)

HUW: Lizard.

SINEAD: What?

HUW: They gave me lizard for breakfast.
(*Silence.*)

SINEAD: I need some answers Huw. I'm going to Wales.

HUW: We came from whales.

SINEAD: You did. Not me.

HUW: We started out as whales then we got smaller and smaller and then we grew arms and legs and came out of the water and that was it. We came from whales.
(*Pause.*

SINEAD takes a deep breath.)

SINEAD: I'm going to have your baby. I tried to tell you…
…… There are things I need to UNDERSTAND! Where's Llareggub?

HUW: (*Stifling tears.*) Bugger all backwards.
(*Silence.*)

SINEAD: I read the play in hospital. What really happened to your first wife?

HUW: (*Through tears.*) For years I was huddled in the dark of unmemory, furled in a wrap of deepest dead-eye sleep alone and whacky, shipwrecked and accused: a minion of Doctor Crippen. But only Dylan has said this with his minnow's mind and wild whirling words of Welsh windbaggery!

SINEAD: Huw… (*Pause.*) I'm going to have a baby. I need some answers. For all of us. (*Pause.*) Did you lie about your wife? Is she still alive? Tell me?

HUW: I can't.

SINEAD: Why?

HUW: I'm nothing. Not even a fly on a cow's nose. I'm a Welshman who only speaks English. I don't belong anywhere. I'm evicted. Finished.
(*HUW turns to look at her but is speechless.*)

SINEAD: You didn't mean to hurt me?
(*HUW is bottling up tears and shakes his head: 'No'.*)
And if you'd known I was pregnant you wouldn't have dreamed of touching me.
(*HUW shakes his head: 'No'.*)
We can put all this behind us. But I need to know!
To save you! Where's Milk Wood?
(*Silence.*
He is crying.)
Alright Huw. It'll be alright.
(*She kisses him.*
Lights down.)

Scene 10

On board ship for Liverpool

Sound of a ship's hooter etc.

SINEAD is standing at the prow of the ship.

SINEAD: And so I sailed out of New York for Liverpool, Wales and Milk Wood. I had a mission! I was going to save my husband from whatever it was this play was doing to him and give me and my baby a future.
And I stood proud at prow day after day, steadfast. A few days out and we hit a bank of mist. It was at dusk. After about an hour in this mist I became aware of someone standing beside me.
(*ROGER stands beside her.*
He wears glasses.)

ROGER: Hello.

SINEAD: Hello.

ROGER: My name is Roger.

SINEAD: Roger.

ROGER: I've seen you standing here at the front of the ship day after day. You're like someone with a mission. As if you're willing the land to you.

SINEAD: Well in a way that's true. My husband is…um…ill in New York. He's from Wales and I'm going back there to see if I can find any relatives of his.

ROGER: O.

SINEAD: O what?

ROGER: You're married.

SINEAD: I am, yes!

ROGER: O well.

(*Pause.*)

SINEAD: (*A little mischievously.*) Were you wanting to make a pass at me?

ROGER: I'm sorry. You've got…

SINEAD: Lovely eyes. I know. Well…all the better to see through you with.

ROGER: I'm sorry. Excuse me…

(*He begins to go.*)

SINEAD: It's alright! You don't need to go!

(*Pause.*)

ROGER: What part of Wales are you going to?

SINEAD: Why? Do you know it?

ROGER: O yes. I'm Welsh.

SINEAD: You don't sound it.

ROGER: (*Suddenly sounds very Welsh.*) Aha! And that is SO important to the Welsh. Well observed! You've got me onto my favourite subject: when are the Welsh Welsh and are the sounds a Welshman makes more important than the sense he makes with them?

SINEAD: You sound Welsh now.

ROGER: A professional! On the other hand, do I? Perhaps to the Irish or my students. But to the Welsh-speaking Welsh I only sound like a certain kind of Welshman.

A Welshman without the language of Welsh. That's what
I'm saying. A Welshman who speaks Welsh makes a
different sound.

SINEAD: Well he would from someone speaking English!

ROGER: But it leaves the Welsh without Welsh in a kind of
limbo. Part of a nation they can't belong to. As though
they were evicted.

(*SINEAD gasps.*)

SINEAD: That's what Huw said!

ROGER: Living on the street outside their own home.
Cast out and always wanting to come back. This is
typical of the ex-pat Welshman like me: always returning
like it's a disease. It makes us seem ill-defined; without
purpose; shifty: the Taffy!

SINEAD: This sounds so much like my husband's problem!

ROGER: It's almost like a curse.

(*SINEAD gasps.*)

In my case made more acute by being a Welshman
called Roger.

SINEAD: You said 'curse'!

ROGER: O yes. And it infects everything. And you hear a
Welshman abroad and he wants to SOUND as Welsh as
possible. Do you know the play *Under Milk Wood*?

SINEAD: Yu...yes.

ROGER: It's mostly sound with little apparent substance.
I know! I teach it!

SINEAD: You teach that play?

ROGER: The Life and Works of Dylan Thomas. SOUND,
mun! You see? The word is even in the way we express
ourselves.

(*SINEAD's mouth falls open.*)

Are you alright?

SINEAD: It's because of him and that play that I'm going...
Look, I can't tell you now, it's a long story, my husband
is the model for one of the characters in *Under Milk
Wood*...

ROGER: (*Shocked.*) Which one?

SINEAD: Mr Pugh.

ROGER: Pugh! So! He's in New York! I've traced most of the models! Well, well...

SINEAD: What about Mrs Pugh? Is she still alive?

ROGER: He lied didn't he?

SINEAD: How d'you know?

ROGER: He's Welsh, mun!

SINEAD: Don't say that! Is she still alive?

ROGER: Was he drunk?

SINEAD: Who?

ROGER: Huw! When he lied.

SINEAD: Well...yes...but...

ROGER: It's alright. It's a familiar pattern.

SINEAD: Is she still alive?

(*Pause.*)

ROGER: Mrs Pugh was a large woman who, after he left lived almost entirely in her single bed. One morning not long after his departure, adrift in her loneliness and the meanness of her thin bed, her memory of her size and the care needed to manoeuvre her bulk in her narrow world, abandoned her and she fell out and died.
They said it was a broken heart. But it was a broken chamber pot. It disembowelled her.

SINEAD: Poor woman!

ROGER: The undertaker said it was like cleaning out a cowshed.

(*Pause.*)

SINEAD: Urrrrghhh! That's disgusting!

ROGER: Yes. Probably a Welsh joke. But, she is certainly dead. Listen: Hugh's lie would have been intended to be without great consequence.

(*Pause.*)

SINEAD: It must be in the nature of a man who can allow himself to be cursed by a mere play that he'll tell a great lie and consider it inconsequential whereas it is a most serious thing to a woman who has had to leave her past because of the on-going cruelty of her history.

ROGER: Is this how you want to go back to him?
To torment him with his lie? I think not. Forget it. Instead, flush out the curse and help him!

SINEAD: (*Tearfully.*) I must! I know! Where is the town of
    the play?

ROGER: Nowhere!

SINEAD: (*Horrified.*) What? No! Don't say that!

ROGER: It's an amalgam – of Swansea, Laugharn and New
    Quay. The three sea-places Dylan lived in in Wales.
    (*Pause.*) What you need is night.

SINEAD: Night?

ROGER: The play is written in three sections: morning,
    day and night. But Dylan died before he could really
    work on the night section and as a result, nothing was
    decided. And after he died, those who knew him best –
    his drinking friends – people like Pugh, became
    like the shipwrecked: all at sea, living in a mist of
    indecision, a greater mood of indecision than was
    already the bane of their lives, uncertain about who
    they were or where they were going. Because he died
    so suddenly. There is just one clue that may help you.
    Right at the end of the play as we come towards night,
    First Voice says:
    'In the warm white book of Llaregyb you will find the
    little maps of the island of their contentment.'
    You must go to the book.

SINEAD: But where is it? Where is the White Book of
    Llareggub?

ROGER: You will find it in New Quay. In the Black
    Lion Hotel.

SINEAD: The Black Lion Hotel. How will I get
    there?
    (*ROGER goes and his voice becomes an echo – on tape.*)

VOICE OF ROGER: In Liverpool, get a train for
    Aberystwyth. You will have to change probably at Crewe
    and Shrewsbury. In Aberystwyth get a bus to Aberaeron
    where you can get another bus to Llanarth. In Llanarth
    you must go to the Post Office and ask for Ivor Bach and
    he will take you by taxi to New Quay. To New Quay and
    The Black Lion Hotel.

Scene 11

Black Lion Hotel, New Quay

Behind the bar is CAPTAIN SIGHTLESS SMITH. He wears blanked off glasses.

SMITH: O sad is me for I smell but cannot see the sea. But I can hear the lap of tide like a cat licking milk and am thus sound in my sightlessness.

(*SINEAD comes on.*)

Captain Sightless Smith old sod of the sea at your service.

SINEAD: Sightless? (*Pause.*) You're Captain Cat!

SMITH: And you are Irish – from the North but a Catholic because there is some South in there too. And now you live in America where you went to flee the inequalities of life in the six lost counties of Ulster. But you have come to Wales on a mission. To New Quay. To The Black Lion Hotel to ask for...

SINEAD: (*Breathless.*) The White Book...

SMITH: O you sweet breath of dawn! You beautiful enquirer. I thought we were done for for only the non-Welsh can lay their hands upon the book! And I don't mean the Welsh of Non the saintly mother of David our Saint beyond all sainthood, but those who are not Welsh but altogether something else! Only the non-Welsh with a mission to save the soul of one washed away in the flood of Dylan's imagination!

SINEAD: Where is it! Is it here?

SMITH: No, no! Buried!

SINEAD: (*Horrified.*) Buried? But where!

SMITH: You must go to the hill above the Old Quarry. On the hillside you will find an old oak. You can't miss it. On the trunk is carved a heart and inside the heart the words: Dylan loves Caitlin. Stand there at midnight tonight! You'll hear the drunken boys roll out of the bars...

(*We hear the distant sounds of late night revellers.*)

HUW: ...peeing their way to their fish and chips and vomit in the vicar's lavender and the high pitched cries of the laughing girls as their skirts get blown waist high by no-good boyos. And you will hear the bell toll for midnight. (*We hear the bell toll.*) Beneath this tree there is a stone and beneath the stone is the book. At midnight... (*We hear the faint sound of sea and seagulls and begin to hear the low murmur of The Voices as midnight begins to chime and throughout the chiming The Voices get louder and SINEAD looks about her fearfully and wraps her coat around her. Then we hear the sound of wind and SINEAD gasps and cowers. There may even be thunder and crashing lightning and SINEAD cries out almost hopelessly.*)

VOICE OF SMITH: ...pick up the stone and lift the book. (*She does this as he speaks.*) Open the book and within the shortest time you will feel his breath...

SINEAD: (*Fearful.*) Who!

VOICE OF SMITH: And he will be there.

SINEAD: (*Opening book.*) Who!

VOICE OF DYLAN'S GHOST: Listen!
(*Everything suddenly goes quiet.
The VOICE OF DYLAN'S GHOST should echo loudly.
SINEAD gasps looking around her but can see nothing.*)
I am here on this hill and on every dewed blade of grass in every moled or moleless hole on every rabbit run track, sliding up the back of every sly besmooched lover licking their lips with a breath of lavender.

SINEAD: Who are you?

VOICE OF DYLAN'S GHOST: I am Dylan. You have come because of Huw.

SINEAD: Yes! Help me! Help Huw!
(*Silence.
After a moment we hear sobbing coming from the VOICE OF DYLAN'S GHOST.*)

VOICE OF DYLAN'S GHOST: (*Sadly.*) It was only a play. The drinkers of the West Wales world hated me just as the melancholic of Wales have always hated their best as

though the best come to haunt them with their less than
bestness and they would mix envy with their grog.
I would carouse with them till the early hours with
Caitlin my stalwart bride and drinking pal beside me
and they would hang from every little ditty I'd sing
and every tale from the fabled Big Apple I'd bite.
But in the days without me in their little gangs huddling
useless with no future or past they would curse my
world-wiseness and say as the Welsh do: who does he
think he is? Is he a philosopher or a surgeon or a
politician? No! HE IS A WIND BAG!

SINEAD: But what about Huw?!

VOICE OF DYLAN'S GHOST: O I mourn for Huw if the
dead can mourn though they should because it's in their
gift to know the sad sounds of eternity. One night, to
brag a worldliness, he said of his middle-aged wife who
would moan about his moonlighting, that one morning
he'll do for her like Crippen did for his. I'd had enough
of this two-faced flounder! And so, as is the way with
sailors of dreams – the writers of the world – I repaid
him for his niggardly predispositions. But I didn't know
I was going to die! It was meant as a literary joke that
I would put right in the rewriting. Close the book and all
will be well!

SINEAD: No! Not yet! The curse! You must take it away!
The play cursed him!

VOICE OF DYLAN'S GHOST: The play did not curse
him, it cursed ME! I turn in my grave when I think how
the English have made of me, through that play, the final
Welshman! It's kept the Welsh of Welshless Wales down
while it's made a bomb in the States! When I was out
there I drank gallons in my loneliness. It made me
cowardly and, becoming a coward in this way I drank
more. I would want to come back but there is never
anything but unwantedness to come back to for cowards!
Close the book and remember me not for the play but
for the poems; as a poet of the soul!

SINEAD: But what about Huw's curse?!

VOICE OF DYLAN'S GHOST: It's his cowardice! Close the book! I'm in pain!
(*SINEAD closes the book. There is a W-O-O-O-O-S-S-S-H-H-H as VOICE OF DYLAN'S GHOST leaves. SINEAD lets out a cry of joy.*
Lights down.)

Scene 12

Hospital

HUW is standing looking calmer.

SINEAD comes on.

Silence.

HUW: There was a young woman from Limerick
   Who thought she was going to be heartsick
   So she went to the Wood
   And there understood.
   (*SINEAD comes to HUW.*)
SINEAD: Huw. If I said your curse was your cowardice, would you hate me?
HUW: No. (*Pause.*) I've known.
SINEAD: You've known?
HUW: Yes.
SINEAD: So why didn't you say so?
HUW: Because I was too cowardly to. Until now.
   (*Pause.*
   They look at each other in silence for a moment.)
   Forgive me?
   (*Silence.*
   SINEAD goes to HUW. They embrace.
   Lights down.)

   The End.

POEMS

Theatre of Death

The stage is our being, Federico
And for that the Ghosts
That describe the world can be given by us
For an hour or so to life.

We, then, the playwrights should do better
Than merely direct actors
To ape the flaws of their being
Which mimics, like dying does, the acting of others.

We must be fearless, Federico
And dismiss from the stage
Life's posturings and vainglorious intentions
And remake Theatre in Death.

In that Theatre, the actor lives
The man in the actor delivering
What we the playwrights make
Of the unmitigated life of the man.

Let others squander
The incomparable virtues of this space
Hauling cadavers around
An otherwise unimportant place.

Theatre is a music of Death, Federico,
But not orchestrating murder or plague
Or the degeneration of living –
It is music beyond the use of time.

Life's theatre is dead.
Only Death's theatre is living
We the playwrights must employ
The expertise of Ghosts before our dying.

On First Meeting Edward Bond

the wind torn from the well
the city torn from the wind
streets scorched velveteen
arms dislocated form arms against you
schooling tears
I went to Yenan

the flower of youth gathers by the Yellow River
beyond the horizon the universities of the enemy
they send 100 carts to steal our wheat
we sent the carts back with their dead
we put fire to the burners
learned well in Yenan

Blues

Looking out from here
I see a blue that captures
Every blue and meaning of blue
And blue meaning: a sea
Shoreless and of night sky
Possibilities. In this lazuli
Of layered blue layered
With colour dissected time
My heart chokes, my eyes
Tear lashed.

I cannot speak of the people
Who people my eyes and heart
Who people the blue
Who pigment my life with blue
Who make blue love,
I can only speak of the shoreless
Sea I look out from here onto.

O the sea horses sad!
Is it my old eyes or
Is that my daughter out there
On that wave, waving
Her red and blood-rusted ribbon?
My beautiful rust-departed daughter.

Reckonings

Odysseus refinding Ithaca
his galley green
with work and journeying
and, like the sun, high
and optimistically anchored
found ashore
in the subtext of his homecoming
that depth of disappointment
which makes despair of sadness.

All that work of journeying!
The struggle to reinvent
his life; all that purpose
to be denied by the deniers
of purpose: the pilferers of the politics
those sly-handed
suitors for the mantle of influence.

Who are they these fortune hunters?
The farmers of Ithaca!
The workers now suited
seduced by the smooth-tongued
sons of princes, the corrupted.

Odysseus says:
let me weep for the loss of meaning
then let there be blood, cleansing blood.
For Odysseus knows
there can be no theft of the politic
without a reckoning.

And Telemachus, the son,
up to his gut in the gore of the purge
now optimistically anchored
is reborn for the re-establishing.

Spring

Again the soldiers fill the valley.
Driven by necessity
The men forge cannon
And the women spin cloth for uniforms
in their parlours.
Soon, the snowdrops.
Young wives weave boots from palmetto fronds
And aunts save their piss
For the nitre that makes
The gunpowder that makes
All the sloshing about in tears
And furnishes the men in war.

Soon, the primrose.
The children in the little games
Have nothing to say of war
But die.
The older girls knit socks for the dying.
The young men cut up the bodies playfully
Notwithstanding history's immanence
And not yet fearful of the waking
From their drunk and bloody spell.

Soon, the cuckoo
And the cuckoo-flower;
Cuckoo-pint:
Arum and wake-robin
And navelwort and pennywort
And all the crazy flowering
Of even the monocotyledonous plants!
And in the lacunae between horrors
Much is fulfilled as the comedian entertains
And flap the colours of war hanging
From rope made of Spanish moss.